Housetraining FOR DUMMIES

by Susan McCullough

WILEY

Wiley Publishing, Inc.

Housetraining For Dummies®

Published by
Wiley Publishing, Inc.
111 River Street
Hoboken, NJ 07030
www.wiley.com

About the Author

Susan McCullough writes about dogs and companion animals for magazines and newspapers all over the United States. Her work has appeared in outlets such as *Family Circle, The Washington Post, Modern Maturity, Woman's DayMoms on Call, Woman's World, Dog World, Cats* magazine, *Animal Fair, PetLife,* and *Popular Dogs.*

Susan is a member of the Dog Writers Association of America, the Cat Writers Association, and the American Society of Journalists and Authors. She is a winner of the DWAA's Maxwell Medallion for outstanding feature writing in the year 2000 and was a finalist for a Maxwell in 1999.

When she's not writing or hanging out with friends and family (both two-legged and four-legged), Susan counsels puzzled people on how to deal with canine potty problems and other dog-related quandaries. She lives in Vienna, Virginia, with her husband, Stan Chappell; their daughter, Julie Chappell, and the family's energetic Shetland sheepdog, Cory.

Dedication

To Cory Poldark McChappell, CM, HG

(Canine Muse, Housetraining Genius)

Author's Acknowledgments

No man is an island, and no author is, either. I want to thank everyone who made this book possible, including:

- ✔ The editors at Hungry Minds — Susanna Thomas, Scott Prentzas, Kelly Ewing, Mike Singer, and Kira Sexton — who all helped to calm my first-time author jitters and make this book the best it could be;

- ✔ Kim Campbell Thornton, technical reviewer, whose expertise made this a better book and helped me breathe easier;

- ✔ Lynn Whittaker, my agent, who is the writer's champion every author longs for;

- ✔ All the people who shared their dogs' housetraining stories with me, and all the experts who let me pick their brains;

- ✔ And most of all: Stan Chappell, my husband, and Julie Chappell, my daughter — for believing in me and being there for me every step of the way.

Publisher's Acknowledgments

We're proud of this book; please send us your comments through our online registration form located at www.dummies.com/register.

Some of the people who helped bring this book to market include the following:

Acquisitions, Editorial, and Media Development

Project Editor: Kelly Ewing

Associate Editor: Kira Sexton

Editorial Supervisor: Michelle Hacker

General Reviewer:
Kim Campbell Thornton

Illustrator: Marcia Schlehr

Cover Photos: ©Kent Dannen

Production

Project Coordinator: Nancee Reeves

Layout and Graphics: Joyce Haughey
Jackie Nicholas, Jacque Schneider,
Mary J. Virgin, Erin Zeltner

Proofreaders: Laura Albert,
John Greenough, Andy Hollandbeck,
Susan Moritz

Indexer: TECHBOOKS Production
Services

General and Administrative
Diane Graves Steele, Vice President and Publisher, Consumer Dummies
Joyce Pepple, Acquisitions Director, Consumer Dummies
Kristin A. Cocks, Product Development Director, Consumer Dummies
Michael Spring, Vice President and Publisher, Travel
Brice Gosnell, Associate Publisher, Travel
Suzanne Jannetta, Editorial Director, Travel

Publishing for Technology Dummies
Richard Swadley, Vice President and Executive Group Publisher
Andy Cummings, Vice President and Publisher

Composition Services
Gerry Fahey, Vice President of Production Services
Debbie Stailey, Director of Composition Services

Contents at a Glance

Cartoons at a Glance

By Rich Tennant

"We've trained him to 'go on command'. Currently, the command is, 'RALPH-GRAB THE DOG BEFORE HE GOES ON THE CARPET'."

page 39

page 87

"WE'VE HAD SOME BEHAVIOR PROBLEMS SINCE GETTING 'SNOWBALL', BUT WITH PATIENCE, REPETITION, AND GENTLE DISCIPLINE, I'VE BEEN ABLE TO 'BREAK' ROGER OF MOST OF THEM."

page 133

"You know, you're never going to get that dog to do its business in your remote control dump truck."

page 7

"Down Skippy, down !! Mike has tried so hard to socialize this dog so we can have people over without being embarrassed, but evidently he needs a few more lessons."

page 163

Cartoon Information:
Fax: 978-546-7747
E-Mail: richtennant@the5thwave.com
World Wide Web: www.the5thwave.com

Table of Contents

Introduction

*W*hen you brought home that adorable little puppy or noble-looking adult dog, you undoubtedly were looking forward to a lifetime of love, devotion, and companionship. Maybe you wanted a dog to jog with in the morning, curl up at your feet in the evening, and/or talk to during the day. Perhaps you were looking forward to heaping lots of unconditional love upon a hard-luck rescue dog who hadn't known such love before. Or maybe you remembered watching *Lassie* when you were a kid, and were hoping your new family member could be the same sort of friend-of-a-lifetime that the famous collie was for little Timmy.

Every new relationship between a person and a dog starts out with at least a little bit of fantasizing on the part of the person. Soon thereafter, though, reality intrudes upon those fantasies. All too often, that intrusion takes the form of a puddle or pile deposited on the floor of your home.

The puddle is yucky. The pile stinks. Both leave stains. And you are totally grossed out.

It's tough to love a pooch who turns your nicely decorated home into a canine outhouse. But this doesn't have to happen. You just need to teach your dog proper potty manners. You need to housetrain him.

By housetraining your canine companion, you'll be teaching him what parents teach when potty-training their human children. Just as potty-trained children have learned to eliminate only in the toilet, a house-trained dog has learned to eliminate only in the places where his people want him to do those things. And, more than likely, a housetrained dog does that eliminating at only those times that his people permit him to do so.

When your dog is housetrained, your life (and his) becomes a whole lot easier and immeasurably more satisfying. Gone will be the doggie accidents, stains, and smells that keep professional carpet cleaners in business, but all too often ruin the precious bonds between dogs and their people.

About This Book

I've written *Housetraining For Dummies* to make sure that you and your dog maintain those bonds. This reference book is designed to help you prevent your pooch from developing potty problems or to solve any problems he's already got.

Whether you have a brand-new puppy who's piddling on your equally new Oriental rug . . . a fractious adolescent male dog who's practicing leg-lifts (and subsequent anointings) right next to your antique loveseat . . . a matronly female dog who's wetting her bed while she sleeps . . . or simply a pooch who never seems to know what he's supposed to do when you take him out — no matter what your dog's bathroom issues are, this book can help you sort them out and resolve them.

And you don't necessarily have to read the book from start to finish to teach your canine companion proper potty deportment. This is a book without rules. If you want to know everything and then some about housetraining, begin reading here and plow through to the end. But if you've got a specific concern, such as wanting to teach your dog to tell you when he needs to go out, skip the preliminaries, look over the table of contents, and proceed to the chapter that will tell you exactly what you want to know.

How This Book Is Organized

Anyone who reads *Housetraining For Dummies* can teach her dog basic bathroom manners. Here's how I've organized the book to help you toilet-train your own special pooch.

Part 1: Mastering the Preliminaries

This part is where you find out what you need to know about your dog (and about yourself) before you start housetraining your canine companion. You find out exactly what housetraining is and get quick introductions to the two housetraining methods covered in this book. You also read about the basic canine instincts that make housetraining possible in the first place and begin to understand the approach you need to take if your own housetraining venture is to succeed.

Part II: Gearing Up

Before you start housetraining your dog, you need the proper equipment. In this part, you discover exactly what gear you need — from leashes to pooper-scoopers to dog litter — to do the housetraining job right, no matter which method you choose.

Part III: Getting Down to the Nitty-Gritty

Once you master the preliminaries and acquire the right gear, you're ready to begin housetraining in earnest. This part shows you exactly how to teach your dog to eliminate where and when you want him to. You also find out how to teach your dog some advanced bathroom manners, such as asking to go out and maybe even eliminating on command. In addition, you get a head start on dealing with housetraining lapses: those times when, despite all your efforts, your dog appears to have forgotten where and when he's supposed to do his business.

Part IV: Making the Nutrition Connection

In order to regulate what comes out of your dog's body, you need to regulate what you put into him beforehand. In this part of the book, you find out why good nutrition is essential to successful housetraining, and how to make your dog's dining experiences the best they can possibly be.

Part V: The Part of Tens

This part is where you can learn more about how to solve housetraining problems — and, hopefully, have some fun while you're learning. You discover that housetraining lapses often have nothing to do with your dog's toileting tactics, but instead indicate that there's some other problem, either with his behavior or with his body. You also get the scoop on common housetraining mistakes and how to prevent them. Finally, you discover some World Wide Web sites that provide a goldmine of information not only about housetraining, but also about other aspects of dog training, behavior, and health.

Icons Used in This Book

To make this book easier to read and simpler to use, I include some icons that can help you find and fathom key ideas and information.

This icon calls attention to ideas or items that are especially helpful when housetraining your dog.

Perhaps you want the full scoop on why dens are such a big part of most dogs' lives, not to mention your ability to housetrain your pooch successfully. This icon flags such information for you. On the other hand, if you just want to understand the basic concepts, sidestep this icon and move on.

This icon reminds you of similar or related information that's contained elsewhere in the book or guides you to a more extensive discussion of the topic in another chapter.

This icon denotes information that's so critical to successful house-training that you should read it more than once — just to ensure that you remember it as you potty-train your own pooch.

This icon flags dangers to your dog's health or well-being.

Sometimes an apparent housetraining problem is really a medical problem that demands a veterinarian's attention. This icon flags such problems for you.

Conventions Used in This Book

In any book that deals with bodily wastes, it's difficult to sound genteel. So I won't even try. Generally, I refer to a dog's waste byproducts as *poop* and *pee,* rather than use oh-so-coy terms such as *number one* and *number two.* And I usually characterize the acts of eliminating as *pooping* or *peeing* — although occasionally I substitute other terms just for the sake of variety.

But while this book makes no bones about what the dog is doing, other terms commonly used in discussions of doggie bathroom manners won't appear here. For example, you won't see the words *housebreak, housebreaking,* or *housebroken* in this book, except when I describe the history of canine toilet training. That's because when you teach your dog to eliminate appropriately, you're not breaking anything. In fact, you're doing quite the opposite: By teaching the dog to poop and pee when and where you want him to, you're building bonds between you. You're laying the foundation for a loving, long-lasting relationship.

In addition to being a neighborhood dog lady who's helped many people housetrain their dogs, I'm also a writer and journalist who specializes in topics related to dogs and other pets. Throughout my career, editors have told me that the correct pronoun to use when referring to an animal is *it.* Till now, I've kept quiet and done what I've been told. But I don't agree with that dictum, and I won't apply it in this book.

Dogs and other animals — even the neutered ones — have clear genders. Moreover, they're living beings and deserve the dignity of being referred to as such. For that reason, I use *he, she, her, him, his* and *hers* to refer to our canine companions. Any of those pronouns apply to both genders unless specifically noted otherwise.

The same principle — that dogs are living individuals — also means that I use the word *who,* not *that,* to refer to our canine companions.

Where to Go from Here

If you haven't acquired your new dog yet, or if he's just arrived, it's best to start reading from the very beginning of this book and work your way through to the end. But if your canine companion has been with you for a while, or if you're just trying to solve a particular puppy potty problem, don't fret. Head to the table of contents and/or to the index, where you find the topic that will help solve your dog's specific housetraining problems.

Finally, this book is meant to be a guide and a reference manual, but not a substitute for the up-close-and-personal advice that other experts such as veterinarians, trainers, and behaviorists give. If the suggestions here don't work for you and your dog, or if you have a question that this book doesn't cover, don't hesitate to contact any of these professionals.

Part I
Mastering the Preliminaries

The 5th Wave By Rich Tennant

"You know, you're never going to get that dog to do its business in your remote control dump truck."

In this part . . .

Congratulations! You're adding a dog to your family. And you're determined to get him started on the right foot by making sure that he's properly housetrained.

In this part, I explain what to expect from a housetrained dog, and how you can work with your dog's instincts to get a leg up (so to speak) on housetraining.

Chapter 1

What Housetraining Is — and Why It Matters

*B*oomer, a three-month-old West Highland Terrier, is delighting his new owner with his puppy antics, but is dismaying her with his tendency to pee all over her new Berber rug. No matter how long it's been since the last time he tinkled outside, he always seems to have something left over with which to anoint the floor covering.

Cory, a five-year-old Shetland Sheepdog, would never pee on a Berber rug — or on any other rug, for that matter. He can be counted on to eliminate three times a day: first thing in the morning, early in the afternoon, and in the evening before bedtime. On the rare occasions that he needs another pit stop, he alerts his owner by going to his leash, which always hangs on the same doorknob in his home, and tapping the leash with his nose.

Molly, another five-year-old Sheltie, is just as good at holding her water as Cory is. Lately, though, Molly hasn't been holding her poop. Her owners have come home from work to find one or two little brown piles gracing their dining room floor. They're not happy about having to do the resulting nightly cleanups, but they don't know how to change Molly's behavior.

Which of these dogs is housetrained? Which ones aren't? In this chapter, you not only find out the answer to that question, but also why housetraining is so important to ensuring that you and your very special pooch live happily together.

Housetraining Defined

To know whether your dog is really housetrained, you need to understand exactly what *housetraining* is. Unfortunately, the dictionary doesn't offer much help here. Mr. Webster and his colleagues appear to be a little bit squeamish, not to mention imprecise, in their attempts to define housetraining. After referring the reader to the entry for *housebreaking* (which is bad enough; after all, you're not teaching your dogs to break anything!), the dictionary writers practically hold their noses and sniff as they proclaim housebreaking to be the act of "[training] an animal or a baby to live in a domestic environment with respect to sanitary habits."

Excuse me? Does this mean that housetraining a puppy requires you to teach little Fido to wash his paws with soap before coming down to dinner? Do Noah W. and company believe that housetraining a dog means directing Spot to use antiperspirant after his daily bath or shower? And do you really consider your toilet-trained human toddlers to be *housebroken?* Of course not. But Webster's definition certainly leaves room for such absurd interpretations.

Defining housetraining requires precision and directness. Simply stated, housetraining is the process in which you teach your dog to eliminate *when* you want him to and *where* you want him to — and to refrain from eliminating at any other time or place.

That definition doesn't allow much room for errors or lapses. And clearly, when measured against those criteria, a dog who consistently does his duty outdoors is fully housetrained. That's not the case, though, with a dog that usually tinkles outdoors or never tinkles outdoors. Housetraining is one of those all-or-nothing cases.

The Human-Canine Love Fest

Approximately 35 million U.S. households have at least one canine in residence. Many of the people who live in these households are those who the American Animal Hospital Association says absolutely dote on their four-legged friends.

According to an AAHA survey, two-thirds of U.S. and Canadian pet owners take their animals to the vet more often than they take themselves to their own doctors. And more than half take time off from work to tend to a sick animal.

Need more evidence of the human-canine love fest? Consider these findings from the same survey:

- ✔ Eighty-four percent of the respondents call themselves their pet's mom or dad;

- ✔ Sixty-two percent of the respondents say they celebrate their pets' birthdays — and 43 percent give the pet a wrapped gift.

- ✔ Sixty-five percent have sung or danced with their pets.

- ✔ Forty-four percent have taken their pets to work with them.

- ✔ Fifty-two percent have cooked special meals for their pet.

On the surface, some of these activities seem ridiculous. Singing to a dog? Dancing with one? Giving the dog a wrapped birthday present?

But there's a very good reason that people engage in all these activities: They feel good. I feel really happy when I sing my inane little "Mr. Puppy" ditty each morning to my housetraining paragon, Cory, the five-year-old Sheltie. (Yup, he's my dog.) I feel equally joyful when he and I dance around to the beat of the B-52's. And I've always loved watching Cory and the other dogs I've known tear into their loosely wrapped birthday gifts.

The pleasure, of course, isn't all you get back from the time, trouble, and love you invest in your dog. You also get back a lot of canine-style affection. That furry body snuggling next to you on the couch, those slurpy doggie kisses on your cheek or fingers, the tennis ball dropped at your feet, the happy tail-wagging and yipping that greet your return home (whether you've been gone for an hour or a month) . . . all that love comes back to you just for taking good care of your canine buddy.

That love comes back without any clauses, caveats, or conditions. Your dog won't say, "I'll love you if you give me a piece of that steak you just grilled" (although he'd surely like a sample). He doesn't withdraw his affections if you fail to bring home a toy from the local pet superstore. He doesn't care whether you're having a bad hair day, the boss trashed your big presentation, or you've had a fight with your spouse. He just loves you, no matter how much or how little you love yourself.

In short, people and dogs have a natural bond. Your dog needs you to take care of him, love him, and to spend time with him. In turn, you probably need for your dog to love you back and to let you see evidence of his love in all his endearing doggie ways.

But although the bond between dogs and people is natural, it's not unbreakable. Between individual people and individual dogs, a lot can happen to unravel the ties of love that would gently bind them together.

Threats to the Bond

A visit to any animal shelter provides heartbreaking evidence of what happens when the bond between dog and person is broken. Behind almost every dog in a shelter is a sad story of loss or abandonment. All too often, a relationship that started out with joy and hope ends up with the owner being disappointed — and the dog facing euthanasia at the shelter or dog pound.

One common cause of a rupture in the bond between a dog and his human is the dog's bathroom behavior. An Internet search easily turns up more than 3,000 Web sites that focus on canine housetraining — a clear indication of how tough this task can be.

Worse, though, are some findings by The Humane Society of the United States. The group has conducted several studies of owners who surrender their dogs to shelters. In at least two studies, housetraining problems emerged near the top of the owners' lists of reasons why they gave up their dogs.

Of course, some people choose to keep their dogs even though the animals haven't learned proper bathroom behavior. However, life can be difficult for the unpottied pooch, even if such a dog manages to remain in his home. The dog who fails Housetraining 101 may find himself spending time alone in the basement, backyard, or the garage, rather than in the living room or family room with his human companions. Such exile does preserve household carpets and furniture, and at least the dog retains his home. Still, banishment to remote areas of the house is a less-than-ideal way to deal with a dog who lacks bathroom manners.

Dogs are highly social beings. Just like their wolf ancestors, dogs are pack animals, and they crave companionship. They're not likely to find such companionship if they're relegated to an area of the house that's far away from the rest of the family. And without such companionship, many dogs will rebel. That rebellion can take the form of other behavioral problems, such as excessive barking, destructive chewing, ear-splitting howling, or even aggression toward people and other dogs. Any of those offenses can break the bonds between dogs and their people, even if their housetraining problems don't.

Moreover, when a dog lacks the companionship he craves, he isn't the only one who loses. The family suffers a loss, too: the unparalleled joy of loving and living with a well-behaved canine companion.

And even if the family doesn't banish its dog, the animal's failure to master housetraining can strain his bond with his people. It's hard to feel good about a pooch who doesn't potty properly. That difficulty increases every time one has to clean up a lapse in bathroom behavior. Some people try to put a positive face on such lapses by saying their dogs are "a little bit housetrained." But that's no better than a dog who's not housetrained at all.

Why Your Dog Can't Be "A Little Bit Housetrained"

Housetraining is an either-or proposition. A dog either *is* housetrained, or she isn't. To say that a dog is "partially trained" or "a little bit house-trained" is like saying that a woman is "partially pregnant" or "a little bit pregnant." None of those terms computes.

This concept is important to remember. Why? Because if you consider your dog to be "a little bit housetrained," you're really saying that he hasn't completely learned proper bathroom manners yet. That means you can't really rely on him to go to the bathroom only where and when you want him to. Until they're totally housetrained, there's always a chance that Lassie will decide to use your Karastan carpet as her toilet, or that Laddie will choose to anoint your mother-in-law's prized Chippendale chair.

And, of course, for some dogs, especially puppies, those chances are way better than even. That's certainly the case with Boomer, the Westie pup who's been using that Berber rug as his own personal potty.

But owners of older dogs like Molly, the Sheltie who's leaving unwelcome little presents in her family's dining room, also are coping with unreliable canines. Molly appears to have forgotten the lessons in bathroom manners her owners taught her years ago — or perhaps she never quite understood those lessons in the first place. It's also possible that Molly doesn't feel well.

Chapter 10 discusses what you should do if your dog appears to have forgotten the fine art of proper canine bathroom behavior. Chapters 14 and 15 focus on why a pooch might pee or poop inappropriately — and what owners can do to solve such problems.

But for now, it's fair to say that while housetraining is an either-or proposition, there's definitely more than one way to teach a dog proper potty behavior.

Two Housetraining Methods

Most people who choose to live with dogs want to be able to regulate their canines' bathroom deportment. They want their dogs to poop and pee where and when *they* (the people) choose.

Fortunately, you can choose between two methods designed to help you achieve this goal. The right choice for you and your dog depends on many factors, some of which relate less to your dog's needs than to your way of living. Table 1-1 can help you decide which method is best for you and your dog.

Table 1-1   Housetraining Methods at a Glance

Method	Pros	Cons	Best For
Indoor	No need to go outside	Messy Takes up space	Tiny dogs Apartment dogs Senior citizens Mobility-impaired people
Outdoor	No messes in house Can do anywhere	Bad weather	Most dogs

Maybe you're one of those lucky people who not only works from home during the day, but also has some nice outdoor places to walk to For you, walking a dog can be a real pleasure — and at times even a sanity saver. For you, a housetraining method that takes you and your dog outdoors is probably an attractive option.

Perhaps, though, you're an elderly person or a mobility-impaired individual who can't get out and around easily. The dog walk that's pure pleasure for your work-at-home neighbor may be pure torture for you. If this description fits you, the ideal housetraining method probably means never having to leave the house. Indoor training may be a better choice.

Or perhaps you live in a high-rise apartment building in the middle of the city. When your canine companion needs a potty break, you can't just snap on the leash, open the front door, and head out for a quick stroll or trip to your dog's designated toilet area. Instead, your route to the great outdoors may require you and your dog to walk to the opposite end of a long hallway, wait for the elevator to stop at your floor, ride down to your building lobby on the elevator, and finally get yourselves to the proper spot outside. And all this time, your dog is expected to hold her water. If you and your dog face such obstacles en route to an outdoor bathroom, you may also want to consider keeping her potty indoors.

Those are just a few examples of how your lifestyle can affect the housetraining method you select for your four-legged friend. This book gives you detailed instructions on how to housetrain your dog no matter which method you choose. The next sections, though, include brief descriptions of the two basic housetraining strategies.

Indoor training

Indoor training involves teaching a dog to eliminate in a potty area located inside your home. The potty area can be some newspapers spread on the floor in one room or a litterbox tucked discreetly into a corner (see Figure 1-1).

A dog who's indoor-trained makes a beeline for those papers or litterbox whenever she feels the urge to eliminate. Once she's finished, cleanup is easy: You just flush the poop down the toilet and throw away the papers or used litter.

Figure 1-1: A dog can use either a litterbox or newspapers for an indoor potty.

Indoor training is a viable housetraining option if, for some reason, it's not practical to take your dog outside to eliminate. It's also worth trying if your adult dog is very small (and if his waste byproducts are very small, too).

But indoor training also carries some disadvantages. It's impractical if your dog is much bigger than toy-sized (think how big those waste byproducts are likely to be!). Moreover, if your canine companion is male, sooner or later he'll probably starting lifting his leg when he pees. When that happens, his ability to aim accurately may decline. Instead of hitting the litterbox or newspaper, your canine leg-lifter may leave a stinky puddle on your bare floor.

Do you want to find out more about how to train your dog to potty indoors? See Chapter 8.

Outdoor training

If the idea of turning part of your house into a canine bathroom doesn't thrill you, you're far from alone. That same lack of enthusiasm is probably the primary reason that millions of dog owners opt to teach their four-legged friends to do their bathroom business outside.

Outdoor training involves teaching a dog to eliminate in a potty area located outside your home. The potty area can be a designated spot in your backyard, or be wherever you allow your dog to do his business.

Outdoor training has plenty of advantages. First and foremost, once your dog knows what he's supposed to do and where he's supposed to do it, you'll never again need to worry about canine waste marring your floors, staining your carpets, or otherwise stinking up your house. You'll also have more floor space to use and enjoy, because you won't have any newspapers or litter pans to get in the way of household foot traffic. Finally, those who choose to walk their dogs outdoors can get some healthful, enjoyable exercise as well as some special bonding time with their canine companions.

But outdoor training carries some disadvantages, too: Ask anyone who's had to go outside with his pooch on a cold or rainy night! Fortunately, a little extra training can go a long way toward alleviating the problem of the pooch who takes too long to do his business during bad weather.

Want to know how to deal with the pooch who won't go in the rain . . . the snow . . . or when it's cold? See Chapters 10 and 14.

Another disadvantage of outdoor training is that it can impose some serious limits on an owner's flexibility. For example, you can't plan to go straight from the office to the local watering hole with your coworkers at the end of the day — at least not without considering the needs of poor Fido, who's waiting at home for a much-needed bathroom break. But there are ways to deal with this potential problem, too.

Do you want to teach your dog to do his business outdoors? Everything you've ever needed to know about outdoor training is in Chapter 9.

Chapter 2

Instincts and Learning

● ●

In This Chapter

▶ Finding out what your dog already knows

▶ Housetraining puppies versus housetraining adults

▶ Discovering what mother dogs teach their puppies

▶ Finding out what dogs learn from each other — and from people

● ●

*W*hen it comes to housetraining your pooch, you're not working with a blank slate. That's because your canine companion probably learned a lot about bathroom behavior before you ever met him — and that's true whether he came to you as a puppy or as an adult dog.

However, some of what your dog has learned about peeing and pooping may not be to your liking. Depending on your dog's background, his knowledge can ease your housetraining efforts or present some un- expected challenges. This chapter can help you understand what your canine companion may already know about proper potty deportment, how he picked up those early potty pointers — and what you'll proba- bly still need to teach him.

Basic Instinct: The Canine Version

No, this isn't about what you think it is. I am not going to discuss the proper use of ice picks, and you're not going to see *any* photos of Sharon Stone — with or without a dog. The instincts being considered here are those canine feelings, drives, and desires that have been with your dog since the moment he was born. They're hard-wired into his very being. No one's taught him the behaviors that result from these instinctive impulses; they just come naturally.

The places your dog chooses to sleep . . . his tendency to hoard things . . . his love of licking your face . . . his delight in fetching objects . . . these and countless other actions and reactions are all inborn. And while some of these instincts don't affect his ability to be housetrained, others greatly affect his capacity to learn proper potty deportment.

Once you find out about some of these inborn impulses, you'll also begin to understand how you can direct them. Some of those directions can help your dog learn to do what you want him to do. That's true not only of housetraining, but also of just about anything else you want your dog to learn.

Puppy Versus Adult

Almost any dog can be housetrained. But the challenges of teaching a puppy to "go potty" may differ from those you encounter if you try to teach the same maneuvers to an adult dog.

If you got your puppy from a reputable breeder, he may already know the rudiments of proper potty behavior. That's because the well-bred pup has had lots of opportunities to learn about keeping clean and getting along with other dogs (and people) — both of which are important prehousetraining skills. A puppy who's nailed those basics will be easier to teach than one who lacks such knowledge.

A lot of breeders go even further. They'll take their puppies outside every morning and after meals, and they'll praise the little guys when they eliminate. If your puppy's breeder has done that (ask when you're interviewing prospective breeders), she's already done some of your dog's housetraining for you. That may also be true of a dog you adopt from a shelter, rescue group, or individual.

But even if your new puppy has aced those preliminary lessons, there's one crucial lesson he's only just starting to learn: the lesson of self-control.

To put it simply, your little guy just can't hold it — at least not for very long. A puppy under the age of 4 months doesn't have a big enough bladder or sufficient muscle control to go more than a couple of hours without eliminating. As he gets older, though, a pup's ability to control himself gradually increases. And by the time he reaches adulthood (at about one year of age), a healthy dog usually has plenty of self-control. In fact, some dogs can hold it for a *very* long time. (See the upcoming sidebar "How long can a dog hold it?")

However, even a dog who appears to have an iron bladder isn't necessarily housetrained. The fact that he *can* hold it doesn't necessarily mean that he *will* hold it. That's because an adult dog may be burdened with mental baggage or just plain bad habits that can create additional obstacles to housetraining.

For example, if you adopted your young adult dog from an animal shelter, her previous owners may not have bothered to housetrain her — or if they did, they may have done a poor job of it. Either way, her failure to master proper potty deportment may well have been what landed her in the shelter in the first place.

Many shelter and rescue dogs have behavioral problems that manifest themselves as inappropriate elimination — for example, the shy dog who rolls over and pees whenever someone stand above her and looks directly at her. Even a dog who's been a model of proper bathroom behavior at one point in her life can later appear to forget what she's been taught.

Not surprisingly, then, housetraining an adult dog is often less straightforward than housetraining a puppy. The grownup pooch who has less-than-stellar bathroom manners often needs to unlearn some bad but well-entrenched habits. The person who lives with such a dog may need to develop his detective skills and figure out why his canine companion keeps making bathroom mistakes. By contrast, all a healthy puppy usually needs to become housetrained is some time to grow and to develop some self-control, and some guidance from you in the meantime.

In any case, though, if you know something about your canine friend's instincts and impulses, you'll have a leg up on your efforts to housetrain him.

How long can a dog hold it?

Some dogs appear to have bladders made of iron. Cory, my five-year-old, 30-pound Sheltie, is one such canine. His already awesome ability to retain his urine seems to increase further when the weather's bad. In short, the more it rains, the longer he seems able to hold it. His current pee-pee retention record stands at a whopping 23 hours, even though my family and I gave him ample opportunity to unload during that time period.

Still, the fact that your dog has an iron bladder doesn't mean he should put it to the test. Most experts say a dog needs a chance to pee at least every eight to ten hours. And for puppies, the standard guideline is that they can hold it for the number of months they've lived. In other words, your three-month-old youngster can only hold it for about three hours, max.

Learning from Mom

Even while he's still with his litter, a puppy is learning a lot about life as a dog. From his littermates, he learns not to bite too hard, if he bites at all. He learns how to jockey for position among his brothers and sisters at feeding time. And he learns a lot about proper bathroom behavior.

According to Char Bebiak, Ralston-Purina's chief dog trainer and animal behaviorist, puppies start learning elimination etiquette from the time they're about four or five weeks old. That's when they have sufficient motor skills to start wandering around the nest where they've been living with their mom, and wandering outside the nest a bit, too.

The mama dog takes advantage of this ability. When the pups indicate they're about to go potty, she uses her nose to push them outside the nest. That way, their poop and pee won't stink up the doggie domicile. If the mama dog and puppies are lucky enough to be residing in the home of a good breeder, several layers of newspaper will be at the other end of the room for the puppies to eliminate upon.

Mom-dogs don't urge their offspring outward just to be canine house-keeping whizzes, though. Their efforts are based on something much more important: a biological drive to survive. That drive is rooted in the wild, where mother wolves are equally intent on making sure that their pups don't eliminate within their dens. The reason? Poop and pee stink — and the smell from either could attract a predator. By eliminating away from the nest, the scent draws a would-be predator away from the den, too.

Back in the domestic realm, a good breeder will reinforce the mama dog's efforts. He's placed the puppies' nest and eating area away from where he wants them to eliminate. After the puppies have eliminated on the newspaper that he's placed on the floor for just that purpose, he whisks the soiled papers away and replaces them with fresh ones.

By seven or eight weeks of age, most puppies have developed enough control to master this first bathroom lesson. They have to poop and pee every couple of hours or so, but they've learned to listen to their bodies, and they can tell when they need to go. When they get those urges, they'll try to scurry away from their den before giving in to that compulsion to squat. This effort to eliminate away from the den signals that a puppy is ready to begin learning the rudiments of housetraining.

Denning Dynamics

The lessons a puppy learns about keeping clean go way beyond what his mom makes him do (see the preceding section). The nest that his mother teaches him to help keep clean is really his first den — and dens are a big deal in the lives of most dogs.

But what exactly is a *den?* Are we talking wood paneling and a wet bar here? Maybe a home theater system and new leather recliner? As the guys in those Hertz car rental commercials say, not exactly.

For a dog, the den is simply an area that he can call his own. Generally, it's a small place that's at least somewhat enclosed on two or three sides but also is open on at least one side. The area may be dark, but it doesn't have to be. What it *does* have to be is a place where the dog feels safe and secure.

When a dog seeks out his den, he echoes the behavior of his wild cousin, the wolf. Wolves make considerable use of dens when raising their young. Mother wolves bring up their pups in dark caves that are hidden from the view of an outsider, but from which the wolf family can see the rest of the world. These caves, or dens, are perfect places to leave a litter of wolf pups when mom goes hunting for food with the rest of the pack.

The domestic dog may not need a den to ensure his physical survival, but his urge to find a den is still very strong (see Figure 2-1). My Sheltie office-mate, Cory, is a case in point. In fact, he's using one of his dens right now. While I've been typing this chapter at the computer atop my desk, he's come into my office and crept under that desk. He's now lying at my feet, protected on two sides by the walls of my office (my desk is in a corner). My legs provide a partial third wall that hides him from the view of others who come into the room. However, he's still got a clear view of anyone else who comes in.

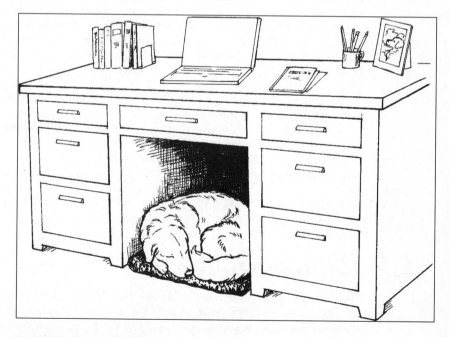

Figure 2-1: Dogs can find dens in unexpected places.

The desk isn't the only den available to Cory, though. He also likes to nap under other tables in the house while my family and I are nearby. And sometimes, while the rest of our family is watching TV, Cory will spend some time in the dog crate he's had since he was a puppy. He also makes a beeline for the crate whenever he sees me wielding the vacuum cleaner, which he hates. On such occasions, I shut the door of the crate before I start my weekly campaign to rid my house of dust bunnies. Inside his crate, with the door shut, Cory waits calmly, knowing that he's safe and secure until I put that big, loud, scary vacuum cleaner away.

Cleanliness Is Next to Dog-liness

So-called *dog people* — humans who are enamored of anything and everything remotely canine — like to say that the word "God" is really "dog" spelled backwards. They may espouse the motto of a magazine called *The Bark*: "Dog is my co-pilot."

These dog people aren't being blasphemous. But their juxtaposition of "God" and "dog" has interesting implications for housetraining. While many people believe that "cleanliness is next to God-liness," most dogs instinctively adhere to the notion that cleanliness is next to "dog-liness." In other words, dogs instinctively want to keep themselves clean.

Sometimes, a dog's definition of cleanliness may differ from yours. You probably don't like the idea of Fido splashing in a mud puddle, but Fido may not mind the mud at all. When it comes to peeing and pooping, though, Fido and most of his canine compatriots draw the line between dirt and cleanliness — and they draw that line right smack in front of their dens.

That's because a normal, healthy dog will do just about anything to avoid having to use his den as a toilet area. The last thing he wants to do is deposit his bodily waste anywhere near his cherished domicile. You can make that impulse work in your favor as you housetrain your dog. That impulse to keep the den clean is the cornerstone of how to teach dogs to poop and pee only where and when you want them to.

The drive to use a den and the drive to avoid soiling that den form the basis of easy, effective housetraining.

Life Without Guilt

Suppose that your dog makes a mistake. Say that he anoints your freshly mopped kitchen floor, or leaves a little pile of poop in the foyer. Do you think he feels bad about it? Do you think he's overcome with remorse? Do you think he even remembers he's done a dirty deed within five minutes of committing the act?

The answers to those questions are no, no, and no. Guilt and remorse are not in your dog's emotional repertoire.

"Now, wait a minute," you say. "When I come home at night from work and see that Fido's peed on the rug, he sure looks to me as though he's feeling guilty. And when I start yelling at him, his ears go back and his tail goes between his legs, and he kind of cringes. And lately he's been running away. He *knows* he's done something wrong."

Fido knows something all right — but that something isn't any realization that he's messed up big time. What he does know is that you're angry. If you're yelling his name, he also figures out pretty quickly that you're angry at *him*. But he doesn't have a clue as to why you're so upset; he's long since forgotten that about his little rug-christening party. All he knows is that you're mad at him, and he's scared of you. Under such circumstances, he takes what looks to him like two prudent courses of action: literally making himself smaller (that's why he's cringing) and beating a hasty retreat.

Does he understand that you don't want him to have any more accidents in the house? Nope. Does he realize that if he didn't have any accidents you wouldn't become angry? No, again. He's just doing everything he can to minimize your wrath and, if that fails, to get away from that wrath — and from you.

Your dog lives a life that's completely free of guilt. He doesn't connect a long-ago action of his with the angry outburst you're having now. That's why yelling at your dog after the fact doesn't teach him anything except to be afraid of you. Time, patience, and consistency are much more likely to get you the results you seek.

Learning by Repetition

Your dog's inability to remember past mistakes doesn't mean that he can't make connections. On the contrary, he's *very* good at linking cause and effect. You can use that linking ability to teach him proper bathroom behavior, or just about anything else you want him to learn. How? With the power of repetition.

In fact, a lot of times your dog will learn something that you haven't planned to teach him. For example, ever since he was a puppy, Cory has liked to watch my daughter Julie walk down the street to school. He can only do this if I lift him up so that he can watch her from the kitchen window. So, from the time he was little, whenever I'd pick him up to watch her go, I'd say "Let's go look out the window." After a couple of weeks, Cory would jump up into my arms whenever I'd suggest looking out the window.

I didn't deliberately teach Cory this little maneuver. I never even thought about it. Nevertheless, I did teach him — by repeating my actions and words day after day, the same way each day. Eventually, he learned that right after I uttered those words and performed those actions, I would pick him up. From there, it was easy for him to anticipate my action by jumping into arms whenever he heard the magic phrase.

While repetition is the key to teaching your dog what you want him to know, you'll need to do less of that repeating if you provide him some sort of incentive for doing the right thing. You can find out more about this positive approach in Chapter 3.

The Need for Attachment

Ever see a litter of young puppies? They tumble over each other constantly and seem to be touching each other all the time. Rarely do you see one puppy consistently go off by himself. Puppies need each other for warmth and companionship; they thrive in each other's company.

But perhaps when you welcomed home your new puppy or dog, you may have made the mistake of having her sleep by herself in the kitchen or basement. If so, you undoubtedly were treated to a night full of heart-rending wails, yips, and howls. Your canine companion didn't like being alone, away from her littermates or the companions of her previous home. Being away from *you* made those already bad feelings seem even worse.

And you all know about the neighborhood dog who is left alone in his owner's backyard all day, every day, and barks his head off — much to the annoyance of those who live nearby. Why does he do it?

Boredom is one reason. Loneliness is another.

Dogs are social animals. If they have a chance to choose between being alone and being with another individual, they'll generally choose the latter.

When dogs make that choice, they're hearkening back to their wild roots. Even today, their wild cousins, the wolves, generally work and play together all the time; their survival depends on staying with the pack. Unlike the wolf, your dog's *physical* survival won't be jeopardized if she's left alone very often, but her emotional well-being may be.

Instinctively, your canine companion knows this. That's why she'll often follow you and other family members from room to room when you're at home. That's also why she'll often position herself somewhere in the house where she can keep track of the comings and goings of every family member.

What does this need for company have to do with housetraining? Plenty. Your dog's desire to be with you not only helps build a precious bond between you, it also helps you keep track of where he is and what he's doing during the housetraining process. No matter how you look at it, your dog's instinctive desire to be close to you is something that you can use when it comes to his housetraining — and any other training.

How Instincts Can Be Thwarted

Instincts play a big role in how quickly your dog masters the art of housetraining. Many puppies learn basic cleanliness and social skills — two important prehousetraining accomplishments — from their mothers and littermates. But what if, for some reason, a puppy doesn't learn those lessons? And how could that happen?

One answer to the latter question is just two words: puppy mills.

Puppy mills are substandard breeding operations in which female dogs are forced to mate as often as possible. Mother and pups are raised in deplorable conditions: I'm talking tiny cages in which these poor animals barely have enough room to turn around. They're also often forced to live knee-deep in their own poop and pee.

Having to live in one's own filth is a surefire way to short-circuit a dog's instinctive drive to do her bathroom business away from her den. She *can't* get away from her den. And — especially if she's a puppy — she can't hold it forever. Sooner or later, she's got to go, and if the den is the only place where she can eliminate, that's where she'll do it. Eventually, she learns to live with it.

What does that mean for housetraining? Simple. A puppy mill dog may take quite awhile to recover her instinct to potty away from her den. And until she does, housetraining will be extremely difficult.

This doesn't mean that a puppy mill pooch can't be housetrained. Plenty of people have persevered until their unfortunate canine companions finally understood where and when it was okay for them to potty. But it takes lots of time and even more patience.

And, unfortunately, many people lack such patience. So, life with their puppy-mill potty delinquent veers off in one of two directions. Either the owners will put up with a dog they say is partially housetrained (which really means the dog isn't housetrained at all). Or, the owners may decide that they can't tolerate the stains, smells, and aggravation of a dog who can't learn basic bathroom manners. They either relegate the dog to remote areas of the house — or worse, get rid of the dog. Any way you look at it, the outcome is unhappy for all concerned.

Clearly, it's better to not take on such problems in the first place. How? By not buying a puppy or dog who comes from a puppy mill. And a surefire way to avoid buying a puppy mill pooch is to avoid buying any puppy who comes from a retail pet store, such as those located in shopping malls.

Sure, those stores are convenient. They've got lots of puppies to choose from, they take credit cards, they don't put you through the third degree the way a lot of breeders do, and you can bring your new dog home the very day you select him.

I know, I know. How can a person be expected to resist any of those cute little pet store puppies, all of whom are waiting for that special someone to bring them home? The answer is, you must, no matter how appealing all those little darlings are. The odds are overwhelming that the puppies being sold at any pet store in a mall came from one or more puppy mills. If you buy such a puppy, you're asking for a lifetime of problems — not just with housetraining, but with the dog's overall health.

You'll up your odds of finding a healthy purebred puppy if you stick to reputable breeders. You'll also help end the nightmare of puppy mills for countless suffering dogs.

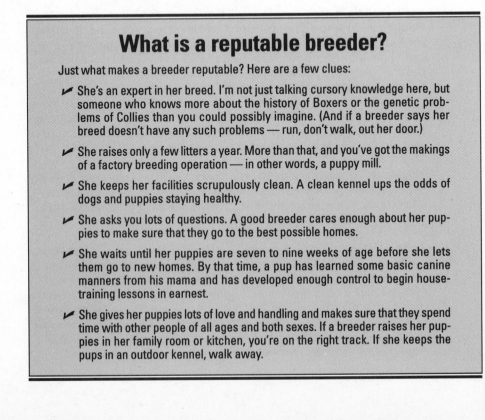

What is a reputable breeder?

Just what makes a breeder reputable? Here are a few clues:

- ✔ She's an expert in her breed. I'm not just talking cursory knowledge here, but someone who knows more about the history of Boxers or the genetic problems of Collies than you could possibly imagine. (And if a breeder says her breed doesn't have any such problems — run, don't walk, out her door.)

- ✔ She raises only a few litters a year. More than that, and you've got the makings of a factory breeding operation — in other words, a puppy mill.

- ✔ She keeps her facilities scrupulously clean. A clean kennel ups the odds of dogs and puppies staying healthy.

- ✔ She asks you lots of questions. A good breeder cares enough about her puppies to make sure that they go to the best possible homes.

- ✔ She waits until her puppies are seven to nine weeks of age before she lets them go to new homes. By that time, a pup has learned some basic canine manners from his mama and has developed enough control to begin housetraining lessons in earnest.

- ✔ She gives her puppies lots of love and handling and makes sure that they spend time with other people of all ages and both sexes. If a breeder raises her puppies in her family room or kitchen, you're on the right track. If she keeps the pups in an outdoor kennel, walk away.

Did you already buy a pet store puppy? Don't despair. Housetraining her will be difficult but not impossible. See Chapter 9, especially the section on "To Crate or Not to Crate."

But suppose that you've opted for an older dog or a mixed breed. Will that dog pose special housetraining challenges?

There's no single answer to that question. Lots of dogs from animal shelters and rescue groups do just fine with housetraining. In fact, quite a few have mastered basic bathroom behavior already. Some, though, may not have. And some may be poorly socialized; they lack the exposure to everyday sights, sounds, and people that enables them to be emotionally well adjusted. That may make it tougher for such a dog to become bonded to you and may also make it tougher for you to help her unlearn some bad bathroom habits.

This certainly does not mean that the dog you adopt from a shelter or a rescue group can't be housetrained. What may be the case, though, is that the task will be a bit more of a challenge than you expected. You'll get a leg up on that challenge, however, if you learn as much as you can about your dog's background *before* you bring him home and start teaching him basic bathroom etiquette.

Chapter 3
The Right Approach

. . . .

In This Chapter

▶ Bringing the right approach to housetraining

▶ Housetraining a dog the modern way

▶ Meeting your dog's needs

. . . .

*Y*our puppy or dog brings plenty to housetraining: a strong instinct to seek out a den, an equally strong instinct to keep that den clean, an ability to learn through repetition, and a desire to bond with you.

But those instincts and desires don't guarantee that he will master the art of proper potty behavior. Just as your dog brings certain attributes to housetraining, so must you. In doing so, you'll develop an approach that will help you housetrain your canine companion quickly and effectively — and also build a solid foundation for a loving, lifelong bond between the two of you.

Housetraining Methods of Yesteryear

Housetraining a dog doesn't have to be difficult. But a generation ago, not many people realized that. At best, housetraining was a difficult undertaking; at worst, it was a total failure. And those failures occurred all too often.

Here's what may have happened. Mom (she was the one who usually got stuck with this task) would see a puddle or pile of poop on the floor. She'd freak — naturally, the little deposit would be gracing a just-mopped kitchen floor or freshly shampooed living room carpet — and go on the warpath to find the canine culprit. When she found him, she'd grab the culprit by the collar, drag him over to the puddle or pile, and yell "Bad dog!" at him. Maybe she'd swat him with a rolled-up newspaper. She might even rub his nose in the object(s) of his offense. The terrified pooch would then creep away, and things would settle down, at least temporarily.

Maybe the dog would eventually figure out what Mom was trying to tell him. Often, though, he wouldn't. And so, the dog would soon have another accident — and the whole miserable cycle would begin again.

Still, the dog was learning something. He learned that the rolled-up newspaper was to be avoided at all costs. He also learned that screaming Moms should be avoided, too.

Back then, people didn't call this cycle of futility *housetraining*. They called it *housebreaking*, as though they were trying to rid dogs of something shameful (see Chapter 1). But these accidents that were so loathsome to people simply resulted from dogs' natural impulses.

Most of the problems people had with potty-training their dogs weren't the dogs' faults — they were the people's faults. People knew very little about the canine instincts that make housetraining and other training easier. All they knew was that they didn't want their dogs to do their business inside our houses.

A 21st-Century Approach

Today, more people understand that to get what they want from their dogs, they have to tune in to what their dogs want. People have discovered a lot about how dogs think and feel and learn. They now know that dogs don't want to poop or pee anywhere near where they sleep and eat. They understand that every canine likes to have a den to call his own. They realize that dogs don't remember what they've done within a very few minutes of having done it. Consistency, patience, and repetition are what's needed to teach a dog what his people want him to know.

Such knowledge enables you to develop a training approach that helps you help your dogs express their instincts in ways that are acceptable to you. In other words, you can train your dog not only to do what you want, but to do what *he* wants, too. You can guide all those instincts into doing things that make you both happy. After you know what your dog can bring to the housetraining process, you just need to realize what you need to bring to that same enterprise. The following sections cover some of the qualities that can help you be the best teacher your dog will ever have.

Thinking like a dog

Any communications theorist, corporate trainer, or psychologist will tell you that in order to persuade someone to do what you want, you have to put yourself in his or her shoes. You have to *become* the individual whom you would like to persuade or teach. You need to imagine his thoughts, and figure out what makes her tick.

That's just as true when you're trying to reach a dog as it is when you're trying to persuade a person. You need to understand the way your dog views the world and relates to it. Put another way, when it comes to housetraining or any other teaching, you'll be miles ahead of the game if you can learn to think like a dog.

When you think like a dog, you realize that it does no good to discipline your dog after he's done something wrong, because he doesn't have a clue as to what that something wrong is. You understand that for some dogs, peeing is much more than an act of elimination — it's a way to communicate with other canines. You realize that the shy little darling who rolls over on her back and dribbles a bit of urine when you come home hasn't mislaid her bathroom manners. Instead, she's paying homage to you, canine-style.

And when you're out walking with your four-legged friend at night and he stops suddenly in the middle of the sidewalk, you realize that he's not being stubborn. More likely, he sees something that scares him. To you, it's just another garbage can — but to him, it's big and bad and dark and menacing. Once you realize what he's feeling and thinking, you can coax him past the object in question, rather than yank on his leash and drag him to you.

You can't succeed with housetraining — or *any* type of dog training — by shoving your wishes down your dog's throat and expecting him to swallow them. Force is not effective; it pits the two of you against each other. Instead, you and your canine companion should be on the same side. You should have a common goal: learning to live happily together.

Thinking positive

No, this section isn't an advertorial for the Reverend Norman Vincent Peale's treatise on *The Power of Positive Thinking*. But frankly, he had a point. There's a whole lot of power in positive thinking — and in positive training.

Think about that old approach to dog training. Basically, it revolved around finding your dog doing something wrong, and punishing him for doing so. But that approach frequently didn't work very well. All too often, dogs didn't know what they were doing wrong, much less how to do something right.

The opposite approach works much better than the negative one. Instead of pouncing on your dog for messing up, you look for him to do the right thing — and when he does (trust me, he will), you reward him lavishly. That reward can come in the form of verbal praise, loving hugs and petting, tasty treats, or even all three. In any case, you take a positive approach.

Are you wondering what kinds of treats to give your dog? Never fear: Just about everything you ever wanted to know about dog treats appears in Chapter 11.

Of course, you don't just wait passively for your dog to do the right thing. You actively guide him into performing the maneuvers you want him to perform, using his own instincts to help him get the idea a little faster. And when he does get the idea, you praise him to the skies. You reward him for doing what you want him to do.

By consistently showing your dog what you want him do and rewarding him for doing it, you're conditioning your dog to do the right thing. You're upping the odds that he will do what you want him to do every time you want him to do it.

Remember reading about Pavlov's dog in junior high science class? The Russian scientist actually got the dog to salivate by giving him a food reward — a treat — every time a bell was rung. The dog learned that the ringing bell would result in his getting a treat, and he began to anticipate getting that treat. He began to look forward to it. He was primed for that food reward, and his mouth began to water.

You don't have to wear a white coat and have a fancy laboratory to condition your dog the same way Pavlov conditioned his. Simply show your pooch what you want and reward him for doing what you've shown him — whether it's the first time he pees in your backyard or the latest instance of his anointing a tree instead of the rug in your bedroom. By giving him that reward, you're letting him know that he's done something that's pleased you, and you give him an incentive to do that something again.

What if he does something wrong? If he pees on your carpet, you clean it up without any comment. If he poops on your brand-new hardwood floor, you whisk the mess away. Period. You don't yell at him. You don't punish him. You certainly don't rub his nose in it. You don't even do the cleaning up in front of him. You just get rid of the mess and move on.

It's important — in fact, it's crucial — to clean up your dog's accidents the right way. For the low-down on the fine art of cleaning up, see Chapter 6.

On the other hand, if you catch your dog in the act of peeing or pooping in the wrong place, you view the situation as a teaching opportunity for you and a learning opportunity for him. You interrupt him in the act and take him to the right place: the place where you have decided he should do his bathroom business.

For specific information on what to do when you see Fido choose the wrong place to potty, see Chapters 8 and 9.

Praise, praise, praise

Don't you love being told you did a great job on that presentation . . . or that you whipped up a fabulous meal . . . or that you look mah-velous, dahling? Of course you do. We all love to be praised; in fact, we thrive on it. Your canine companion is no different. She needs to be praised, too. That's the only way she knows she's doing what you want her to do.

There are ways to praise that are especially effective for dogs. They're designed to duplicate the sounds and gestures dogs make when they're happy. Here are some suggestions:

✔ **Make like a crooner.** When you're praising your pooch, use a sweet-sounding, high-pitched, happy-sounding tone of voice that drips with love. Don't just tell Fido, "Good dog," in a monotone voice, or one that sounds similar to your other communications with him. Exaggerate it, draw it out. Tell him, "Gooooooood dooooooog! What a goooooood boooy you are!

✔ **Look as happy as you sound.** Dogs smile at each other when they're happy — think of a contented dog with a big, panting grin. So when you're happy with what your dog's done, you should smile at him, too. Grin as widely as you can. He'll get the message — and may well smile back at you.

Thinking like a leader

Part of empathizing with your dog and developing the right approach to training is knowing what your dog wants from you.

Sure, he wants a pal. He wants a friend. He wants someone to do things with, to take care of him, to love him, to appreciate him. But he also wants someone to lead him.

This desire for a leader may run counter to all your ideas about friendship. You probably were told during your childhood that it's wrong to be too bossy. And as an adult, you've probably discovered that being a control freak doesn't help you win friends or influence people. Empowerment and democracy are the bywords of the new millennium — the bywords for people, anyway.

But for dogs, it's a different story. And it always has been.

Dogs aren't into democracy. For them, figuring out the hierarchy is the name of the game. They focus on who, literally, is the "top dog" in any social group, and where everyone else, including themselves, stands in relationship to that top dog.

This same dynamic occurs among wolves. They live in groups that scientists call *packs*. Each pack has a leader, known as the *alpha*. The pack works together to find food and take care of the wolf pups, but there's always a clear alpha who leads the way. That alpha decides where to hunt for food and has the privilege of eating first. An alpha male also has sex privileges; he's generally the only guy in the pack allowed to mate with eligible females.

The subordinates adhere to pack etiquette by showing respect for the alpha. They let the alpha go ahead of them while walking. They move in order for the alpha to go past them instead of going around them. They don't object if the alpha decides to help himself to their dinners in addition to his own.

Domestic dogs relate to each other and to their people in much the same way that wolves do. But instead of considering a bunch of wolves or dogs to be his pack, your pooch applies that designation to you and your family. Still, for him there are vital questions to be answered: Who is the alpha? Who is the leader?

It shouldn't be your dog, even if he's the only canine in the pack. Within a human family, a dominant dog is a problem dog. At best, he'll ignore what you tell him to do. At worst, he'll become dangerously aggressive.

You and the other human members of your family should always rank higher in the pack than your dog does. Even the kids need to outrank your canine companion. And it's important to make the respective status of each family member clear as soon as the puppy or dog joins your household.

Now, this doesn't mean you should make like the alpha wolves you see on PBS or Animal Planet or those National Geographic specials. You don't need to aim a death-ray stare at your canine companion, grab him by the scruff of the neck, or roll him over onto his back. Establishing your leadership usually is a lot simpler (and safer) than that, especially if your new dog is a puppy.

You show that you're the leader simply by taking charge. You make the decisions. You decide when he should get his food and when he should get attention, rather than just giving the dog these longed-for items every time he asks for them. You sent the agenda for training, for playtime — for everything.

And when you do so, your dog will be grateful. That's because when you make it clear that you're in charge, your dog knows he can relax. He doesn't have to think about trying to become the Big Kahuna, or worry about protecting his Kahuna-ship. Instead, he can focus on you, his beloved alpha. He can do what he does best: Tune in to you, listen to you, please you, and learn exactly how to do what you want him to do. In other words, he can focus on being a good pack subordinate.

Your dog *wants* you to be his alpha. And by thinking like that alpha, or leader, you can quickly establish a relationship that works well for both of you — which in turn can make housetraining a whole lot easier.

Paying attention to details

Have you ever toilet-trained a human child? If so, you know how important it is to pay attention to seemingly trivial details such as when she last peed in the potty, when he last did a doodoo in his diaper, or what she ate for dinner the night before she has a funny-colored bowel movement.

The same is true when housetraining your dog. During this process, it's important to remember what you fed your four-legged friend and when you did so. It's always good to recall how long it's been since he last peed or pooped. And it's important to know what his pee or poop normally looks like so that you can tell if he might be sick.

In fact, your dog's pee and poop can tell you a lot about his overall health. For more information on how that's the case, see Chapter 15.

Paying attention to details also means taking the time to observe your dog and discover what makes him the unique individual he is. For example, do you know the answers to these questions?

- ✔ Does he lift his leg when he pees? Does he like to lift both legs (one at a time, of course)? Or does he not bother lifting his leg at all?

- ✔ Does he need to eliminate right after he eats, or does he like to wait awhile?

- ✔ Does she like to pee in the same spot all the time, or is she an I'll-do-it-anywhere piddler?

- ✔ Does she circle and sniff before doing her business? Or does she suddenly stop in midstride and do the deed before you quite realize what's happening?

- ✔ Is he a little introvert who sometimes releases some urine when you greet him? Or is he the canine equivalent of *Friends*' Joey Tribbiani: a confident, how-ya-doin' extrovert with a wagging tail and canine grin for everyone he meets?

Think of the stories you tell your human friends about your dog. What are some funny things he's done? How about the sweet things, the poignant things? What are some of his quirks — potty-related and otherwise?

What, you ask, do all these questions have to do with housetraining? Simple. The better you know your dog, the more you'll be able to empathize with him. The more you're able to empathize with him — to think the way he does — the better able you'll be to adjust his housetraining lessons to his unique character and perspective. And the better you're able to fine-tune your housetraining to his unique character, the more effective your housetraining efforts will be.

This personalized — or rather, dog-specific — approach is particularly true with respect to your dog's bathroom habits. By paying attention to what he does when he pees or poops, you'll be in a better position to anticipate when he's going to go — and to intervene if that's going to happen in the wrong place. This ability to anticipate, as you'll soon discover, is a crucial part of successful housetraining.

Want to know how to decode your dog's bathroom style? Check out Chapter 10.

Being consistent

Yes, I know. You've already got so much going on in your oh-so-busy life that there's no way you can possibly remember what color your dog's pee was yesterday or when he last pooped. Believe me, I sympathize. Everyone is on information overload. I, too, have trouble remembering what day it is. Sometimes I even forget that Cory has peed within a mere five minutes of his having done so.

But take heart. There's help for memory-impaired folk: consistency. When applied to housetraining, consistency means having your dog eat, drink, pee, and poop at the same times and places every day. You have your dog's dining and bathroom behavior down to a routine the two of you eventually can do in your sleep.

By adopting a consistent routine for your dog's dining and toileting activities, you'll not only be helping your own memory. You'll also help your dog become housetrained faster — and stay housetrained forever. Dogs learn by repetition. So if you and he are doing the same things at the same time in the same place each day, he'll come to expect that you'll be doing those things.

This consistency affects your dog both physically and mentally. The repetition that you establish in your feeding and housetraining your dog will condition his body as well as his mind. After all, you may be physically conditioned to expect that early morning jog or a second cup of coffee at the same time each day — and without the jog or joe, you don't feel quite right. You don't like that feeling, so you stick with your exercise and/or coffee routine; it becomes a habit.

By establishing similar routines with your dog, you're helping to make housetraining a habit for him. When his body gets used to the routine you set up for him, he'll be primed to poop and pee when and where you want him to.

Don't worry, though. Once your dog is truly housetrained, you won't need to be quite such a fanatic about repetition and consistency. Your dog will have the control he needs to hold it a little longer if your schedule hits an unexpected snag. Still, it's better to keep to at least a semblance of routine, even when your four-legged friend has mastered the art of housetraining.

Creating a schedule

Does it sound as though, in suggesting that consistency is crucial to effective housetraining (see preceding section), I'm practically exhorting you to create a feeding and toileting schedule for your canine-in-housetraining?

What your dog needs from you

If your dog could write a list of what she needs from you to become a happy house-trainee, here's what she might ask for:

✔ Empathy

✔ Optimism

✔ Consistency

✔ Rewards

✔ Attention

✔ Love

And if your canine companion could tell you what would make housetraining tougher for her than it needs to be, here's what she might ask to have removed from your repetoire:

✔ A rolled-up newspaper

✔ A snout full of doodoo

✔ Other punishment

Well, I won't exhort. Not if you've already gotten the idea. But I will say, unequivocally, that having a schedule is a great way to reduce the time it takes your dog to get the hang of housetraining. The training process becomes a whole lot easier if you feed your dog, play with him, and let him eliminate at the same times every single day.

A schedule plays right into your dog's need for consistency and pre-dictability. A schedule also makes it a whole lot easier for you to anticipate when your dog needs to pee and poop and get her to the right place before she has an accident.

There's no one-schedule-fits-all timetable. You should put together something that fits your dog's age, degree of housetraining prowess, and housetraining method you're using. There's more info on how to create this kind of schedule in Chapters 8 and 9.

Laying the foundation

A lot of what I talk about in this chapter may seem to range far afield from the task that confronts you: teaching your dog where and when to eliminate. But nothing could be further from the truth.

That's because Housetraining 101 is probably one of the first — if not *the* first — lesson that you will try to teach your dog. The way you try to show him proper canine potty etiquette lays the foundation for your efforts to teach him other lessons, such as coming when called, sitting when told to, and walking nicely on the leash. What you do now, in this most basic of lessons, will probably set the tone for your relationship with your dog now and in the years ahead. For that reason alone, it's worth taking the time to do the job well.

Part II
Gearing Up

"We've trained him to 'go on command'. Currently, the command is, 'RALPH-GRAB THE DOG BEFORE HE GOES ON THE CARPET'!"

In this part . . .

*B*efore you can begin to housetrain your canine companion, you need to invest in some equipment. This part tells you all you need to know about crates, collars, leashes, clean-up stuff, and other housetraining gear, as well as where to acquire them. You also get a primer on dog-walking — a crucial skill for most housetrained pooches and their people.3.

Chapter 4

The Crate

● ●

In This Chapter

▶ Finding out why dogs love crates

▶ Discovering why crates help housetraining

▶ Choosing the right crate for your dog

▶ Introducing your dog to the crate

● ●

*P*rofessional dog trainers and experienced dog owners have dealt with lots of puppy pee and doggie doo. They've gotten housetraining down to a precise science. And just about every one of them will tell you that there is nothing, absolutely nothing, like a crate for making housetraining easier, quicker, and more effective.

"A crate?" you ask incredulously. "How can that be? Crates are for transporting dogs on airplanes, or maybe for getting the dog out of the way at times when nothing else works. They look like cages. They certainly don't look like any sort of toilet-training device."

But looks can be deceiving. I'm convinced that anyone who's ever used a crate to housetrain a dog would never go back to considering a crate to be nothing more than Fido's home away from home. I've housetrained dogs *with* the help of a crate, and I've housetrained dogs without one. The differences between the two processes are akin to the differences between up and down, or north and south, or winter and summer.

Two Dogs and a Crate

In fact, I housetrained my very first dog without the help of a crate. Molly was an intelligent, thoroughly lovable mixed-breed shelter dog. She was about eight months old when I adopted her in the late 1970s, which was before most trainers and pet owners had discovered how much crates can help with housetraining. Certainly I knew nothing about them, and that lack of knowledge may have made housetraining much tougher for Molly.

That's because, despite her overwhelming eagerness to please and a clear ability to learn, Molly took several months to master her housetraining basics. During that time, I often came home from work to find unwelcome puddles and poop waiting to be cleaned up.

I certainly was a much less experienced, much less knowledgeable owner than I am today, and that may have had something to do with Molly's housetraining challenges. But I'm also convinced that the lack of a crate was the primary reason why teaching basic potty manners to Molly became such a protracted process.

That conviction came about when I acquired the dog who did (and still does) have a crate: Cory, my Sheltie. Cory came to my family and me in the mid-1990s when he was a nine-week-old puppy. He was no more intelligent than Molly was, and a little less eager to please. Nevertheless, he figured out the whole housetraining thing in a matter of weeks, and he's been rock-solid reliable ever since.

The only difference in the way Cory and Molly were housetrained was the crate. But why? How can a simple device that appears to have nothing to do with bathroom behavior make all the difference in the world when it comes to housetraining?

There are two answers to that question. First, most dogs love their crates. Second, this attachment can be a direct link to the two canine instincts that make housetraining possible.

Why Dogs Love Crates

Few objects are more important to a wild or domestic canine than the den: that safe, secure place that the animal can call his own. As I explain in Chapter 2, a den is vital to the health and well-being of wild wolves, and it's almost as important to the domesticated dog.

And a crate makes a perfect doggie den. It's compact. It's cozy inside, or can be made so with some well-chosen crate accessories. It's also dark inside, or can be rendered so by draping a towel or blanket atop the crate. And because it's open on one side but enclosed on the other three, it offers the dog a safe, secure window onto his world.

Even today, Cory — who's long since joined the ranks of properly housetrained canines — still enjoys his crate. Sometimes in the evening, when he's tired of having to share the family room sofa with the human members of his pack, he'll retreat to his crate. He'll also high-tail himself to the crate when he sees me wielding the big, bad, detestable vacuum cleaner.

Dogs like Cory who are introduced to the crate when young soon grow to love these special spaces. And even an older dog can learn to at least tolerate a crate if he's introduced to one properly. Either way, the attachment is well worth cultivating. That's because doing so enables you to tap into a crucial component of your canine companion's denning instinct.

Why Crates Help Housetraining

In the wild, mother wolves train their puppies not to eliminate anywhere near the family den. Similarly, most domestic dogs will do just about anything to avoid peeing or pooping in *their* dens. As I explain in Chapter 2, dogs consider their crates to be their dens, and they quickly learn to hold their pee and poop whenever they're inside those crates. They'll only let the floodgates open when they're outside and away from these structures, which have become their own cherished dens.

Sound simple, doesn't it? It is, but not quite as simple as the foregoing explanation appears. You can't just run out and buy any old crate and then shove your dog into it, thinking that by doing so you'll housetrain him at warp speed. Housetraining, even with a crate, just doesn't work that way. There's a fine art to this task, and it starts with figuring out what size and type of crate to buy for your dog.

Types of Crates

To begin with, there are two basic types of crates to choose from: plastic and wire.

Plastic crates, also known as carriers, are molded two-piece units that are ventilated at the sides and have doors at their fronts. Wire crates are made from panels of welded metal wire that are hinged together. Table 4-1 outlines the pros and cons of each.

Table 4-1	Plastic Versus Wire Crates		
Crate Type	**Pros**	**Cons**	**Best For**
Plastic	More denlike Cheaper Accepted by airlines Adjustable for size	Bulky Can be chewed	Most dogs
Wire	Collapsible More expensive More open	Not okay with airlines Can't be chewed Less denlike	Snub-nosed dogs Dogs who chew

A softer side to crating?

In addition to plastic and wire crates, a third kind of carrier is available to very small dogs: the soft-sided carrier.

These stylish carriers look more like high-fashion luggage for people than portable dens for dogs. They're designed for petite pooches — those dogs who are small enough to travel in an airline cabin with their globe-trotting owners.

How small is small? The Sherpa's Pet Trading Company says a dog who's 18 inches long, 11 inches high and weighs no more than 22 pounds can fit in its large-sized carrier. Such carriers meet airline requirements that carry-on items fit under the seat in front of the human passenger.

But even if your dog's small enough to fit in a soft carrier, don't use it to housetrain her. The housetraining process often involves leaving a dog alone in its crate or carrier, but Sherpa cautions against leaving a dog alone in one of its zipped carriers. Use these soft-sided bags for traveling, but stick with a wire or plastic crate for in-home housetraining.

There are plenty of good reasons to opt for a plastic crate. For one thing, because it's enclosed on three sides (except for the vents), a plastic crate can easily become the snug, dark, cozy den most dogs crave. Another advantage is that plastic crates generally meet airline specifications for pet shipment as baggage or cargo — an important consideration if you plan to travel by air with your canine companion. Finally, plastic crates often cost a little less than wire crates do.

As to any disadvantages of plastic crates, there are probably two or three. One is that plastic crates can take up more than a little storage space. They come in two molded parts that can be nested together, but don't collapse or fold. Consequently, they can't be stashed away in a small space. Another disadvantage is that because they're plastic, such crates are more vulnerable than wire crates to the ravages of canine teeth. Of course, chewing dogs won't get anywhere with wire crates — and that's a big advantage in the wire versus plastic sweepstakes. Another plus for wire crates is that they're totally collapsible, which means that they can be stashed away in tiny places when they're not being used. A third possible advantage is that because wire crates are open all around, your dog can see what's going on when he's lounging in his doggie abode. If your dog doesn't like such openness, you can throw a blanket over the top and sides of the wire crate to create a more enclosed den.

But wire crates carry a couple of disadvantages. For one thing, they're not considered acceptable for airline travel — but if you're not planning to fly with your pooch, that potential problem may be irrelevant. In addition, wire crates tend to be more expensive than their plastic counterparts.

Either type of crate comes in several sizes. For example, one prominent pet retail Web site offers a wire crate in three sizes that range from 24 by 20 by 21 inches to 42 by 26 by 28 inches. The same site offers a plastic crate in five sizes that range from 23 by 17 by 16 inches to 40 by 27 by 30 inches.

Figure 4-1 shows the differences between a wire crate and a plastic crate.

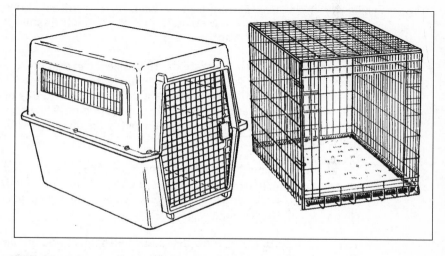

Figure 4-1: Plastic versus wire: The difference is visible.

Ultimately, the decision as to what type of crate to use is a personal and subjective one. There's no right or wrong choice. Your best bet is to assess what your future needs are likely to be and to make an educated guess as to which type of crate your dog is more likely to prefer.

For example, I chose a plastic crate for Cory because he was (and still is) a shy, sensitive little guy whom I thought would be happier having a dark place in which to hide rather than an open-air abode. Other owners — for example, those with snub-nosed dogs who can be prone to breathing difficulties — may choose wire crates. That's because wire crates offer much more ventilation than plastic crates do, making it easier for snub-nosed dogs to breathe.

Adjusting for Size

No matter which type of crate you choose, it's important to keep in mind The Godzilla Factor. The ads and trailers for the 1998 movie about that legendary monster proclaimed that "Size does matter." That proclamation is just as true for crates as it is for oversized cinematic creatures. It's crucial to pick the right size crate for your dog — not just for when he's a puppy, but also for when he's an adult dog.

A correctly sized crate is one that's just large enough for your dog to comfortably stand up, turn around, and lie down. If you get a smaller crate, you'll end up cramping your canine companion. If you opt for a larger crate, you'll be working against your own housetraining efforts. In an overly large crate, a puppy or dog can sleep and eat at one end of the crate and relieve himself at the other. That defeats the whole purpose of using the crate.

Does the need to keep the crate the right size mean that you must buy a new one each time your puppy's size increases significantly? Happily, the answer to that question is no. It's entirely possible to buy one crate that will serve as your dog's den from puppyhood on. The secret: Buy an adult-sized crate and block off some of the inside space while your dog is a puppy.

Start by purchasing the crate that's most likely to be suited to the size your puppy will be when she reaches adulthood. Crate manufacturers label their products with specifications that indicate which size dog each of their crates is meant for.

Then you need to create a divider: a barrier that will wall off part of the crate and can be adjusted as your puppy grows. It's constructed the same way the plate at the back of each drawer of a metal file cabinet is. And it works on the same principle: You slide the divider back as your puppy grows and needs a bigger crate.

To create a divider, cut a piece of cardboard to a size that's just a little wider than the back of your puppy's new plastic crate (see Figure 4-2). Place this cardboard divider inside the crate and insert the divider's sides into the ventilation slots on the side of the crate. You may need to punch holes in the divider sides and use some wire to help fasten the divider to the crate. Then, voilà! — your crate is sized for your puppy's needs, but also will be ready to accommodate your big adult dog when the time comes.

This solution may not work if your puppy likes to chew cardboard. Monitor your canine youngster's chewing habits and remove the divider if he decides that cardboard tastes better than kibble. Make sure, too, that the wire does not protrude inside or outside the crate in any way; you don't want your puppy to chew on the wire or get poked by it.

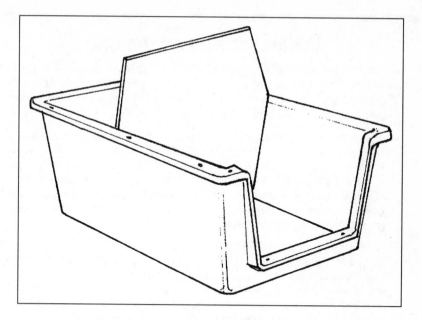

Figure 4-2: How to bring a big crate down to (puppy) size.

Introducing the Crate

Just because the crate makes a nifty doggie den doesn't mean that your dog will view it that way — at least not at first. Instead of considering the crate to be as his own special space, a dog may view it as a doggie prison to which he's received a lifetime sentence. In fact, you can count on his viewing the crate that way if you simply put him in it, shut the door, and leave the room.

To help your canine companion appreciate her crate, introduce her to it immediately but gradually. If possible, start on the very same day you welcome her into your home. Here's what to do:

1. **Let her check out the crate.**

   Begin by letting your puppy walk around the crate and explore it. Then, encourage her to venture within by tossing a tasty treat or toy inside the crate. If she goes in, praise her; if she's hesitant, tell her in a high, happy-sounding voice to go and get the goodies. Don't force her in; let her decide on her own to enter the crate. And when she does, let her know what a good girl she is!

   When you begin introducing the crate to your dog, tie the door open. That way, the door can't accidentally slam shut and spook your canine explorer.

What if she hates the crate?

Not every dog appreciates a crate. An adult dog who's never been inside a crate may think it's a prison, not a haven. A puppy mill pooch who spent his babyhood cramped inside a crate that was too small, and who was forced to eliminate while inside that crate, may not think the crate you've purchased is such a great idea, either.

Either way, a dog who hesitates to enter a crate for the first time probably just needs some patience from you and a clear incentive to give the crate a try. Find a treat that your dog is passionate about and hold it to her nose so that she knows what's being offered. Then, use a high-pitched, happy-sounding tone of voice to encourage her to enter the crate. Once she makes the big step and ventures inside the crate, praise her to the skies. Above all, don't shut the door until she's going in and out of the crate without hesitation.

Some dogs balk when they're left alone in the crate for the first time. If that's the case with your pooch, stay away for just a minute or so after she starts fussing. Then come back into the room and reassure her with a quick "Good girl" or "Good dog." Leave the room again for just a few seconds — and if she stays quiet for that brief time, come back to let her out of the crate and praise her. The important thing here is not to let her out of the crate until she stops fussing.

If you've done your best but there's no way your dog will accept the crate, don't despair. For a few pooches, particularly puppy mill dogs and their offspring, the crate will never be the cozy den it represents to the vast majority of canines. Chapter 10 contains tips for crateless housetraining. Just don't plan on flying your crate-phobic dog anywhere.

2. **Shut the door — but not for very long**.

   Once your puppy repeatedly enters her crate without hesitation, you can shut the door momentarily. Put a treat inside the crate; when your pup enters, quietly shut the door for *just a few seconds*.

3. **Praise her lavishly; then open the door and coax her out.**

   Praise her when she emerges and give her another treat. Do this step repeatedly, gradually increasing the amount of time the door remains closed, until your puppy is able to remain calmly in the crate for about five minutes.

4. **Leave the room.**

   After your puppy can stay calmly in the crate, you can leave the room. Once again, lure her into the crate — but this time, use something more substantial than a treat or two. A safe chew toy or a full meal (in one of her crate dishes) are both good choices.

   Once your pup is in her crate, shut the door quietly and leave the room for about a minute. When you return, see what your puppy's doing. If she's eating her meal or gnawing her chew toy contentedly, leave the room again and come back in a few more minutes. Keep checking until she's finished; when she's done, let her out of the crate and praise her lavishly for her accomplishment!

5. **Build up her tolerance.**

Keep feeding her inside the crate until she's able to stay in it for half an hour; then, try leaving the house for a few minutes, gradually extending the time that you're away.

 Don't view your crate as a puppy warehouse. Even a fully housetrained puppy should spend no more than four or five hours at a time inside his doggie den during the day. If your work schedule makes that impossible, consider hiring a pet sitter or dog walker to give your little darling a much-needed midday potty break and some company — or find a way to do it yourself during your lunch break.

 If your puppy has downed a full meal while she's inside the crate, she'll probably need to pee and/or poop very soon afterward. After she finishes chowing down, take her to a designated puppy potty spot. For more info on choosing and using the potty spot, check out Chapters 8 and 9.

Everyday Crating

Even after your puppy or dog is housetrained, you and your dog will still find the crate useful. In addition to using the crate as a safe place from which to avoid fearsome vacuum cleaners and get himself some space during my family's TV time, Cory uses his crate as an occasional stashing place for toys or treats. (Unfortunately, he soon forgets that he's done so.)

Your dog's crate will also come in handy when you and he travel. Many hotels and motels that generally frown on accommodating animals may cut you a break if you can tell them your dog will be crated. And if you think that you'll only visit pet-friendly hotels — well, think again. If you and your dog find yourselves having to leave your home to outrun a natural disaster such as a hurricane, having a crate can save the day (not to mention your pet's life) when you're both scrambling to find a safe shelter.

The crate also is a safe place for your dog to be when you're both traveling by car — and it's required if you're both traveling by air, and the dog is too large to join you in the passenger cabin.

Any way you look at the crate, though, the bottom line is that a dog who's gotten a good start with one is probably going to have a good start with housetraining and every other kind of training. Showing your dog that his crate is something to love is worth every bit of effort you and he make.

Crating do's and don'ts

Here's a quick set of tips designed to maximize your chances of crate training success:

✔ *Do* consider your dog's needs when choosing a crate.

✔ *Do* make sure the crate is the right size for your dog.

✔ *Do* introduce the crate gradually.

✔ *Don't* let the door slam shut when you first introduce the crate.

✔ *Don't* leave your dog in the crate for more than a few hours at a time.

Crate Accessories

For the sake of your dog's comfort and your own convenience, you may want to invest in a few crate accessories.

Chief among these is some kind of soft mat or flooring for the crate. (You wouldn't want to have to lie down on hard plastic or metal, would you? Neither does your dog.) Crate manufacturers make a variety of mats and carpets to fit their products. They include luxurious items such as cut-to-fit mats made of synthetic sheepskin, or a more basic (but still very comfortable) plastic polyurethane foam mat. Whatever you choose, though, it's a good idea to make sure that your dog's crate mat can be cleaned easily. Machine washability is ideal.

You may also want to buy a couple of dishes that can be attached to the inside of the crate door. Some crates come complete with such dishes, but if yours doesn't, pet manufacturers offer them separately for a reasonable price (around $5 per dish as of winter 2001).

Such dishes will make it easier to feed your dog in his crate — and dining within the crate can help your dog associate the crate with something positive, if he hasn't done so already. Moreover, if you're planning to travel by air with your dog, airlines generally require that there be food and water that the dog can consume inside the crate if the flight lasts longer than a few hours.

Traveling canines and their owners may also appreciate having a *crate dolly*. This contraption is exactly what it sounds like: a metal platform with four wheels and a nylon pull handle. Set your dog and his crate atop the dolly, and you'll be able to whisk him through the airport with ease.

Chapter 5

The Collar and Leash

In This Chapter

▶ Navigating the wide world of dog collars

▶ Conquering the equally wide world of dog leashes

▶ Discovering the right way to walk a dog

▶ Solving dog-walking problems

*U*nless you and Fido plan to spend your entire lives behind four walls, sooner or later, you and he will need to venture into the great outdoors. And if you're like the vast majority of dog owners, you'll opt to housetrain Fido by teaching him to poop and pee outside.

But even if you plan to have your four-legged friend do most of his pottying within your fenced yard, sometimes — such as when you travel — a fenced yard won't be available. Moreover, on any given gorgeous day, you may well get the urge to saunter 'round your neighborhood — and who better to accompany you than your canine companion?

Unfortunately, walking with your dog is not the unfettered affair it used to be. Gone are the days when people and pooches routinely wandered over hill and dale with nothing but love to keep them together. Today, it's generally not a good idea to take your canine companion to public places unless he's on a leash. Between busy streets, dog-phobic people, and proliferating leash laws, you may be risking your finances, your dog's freedom, and both your lives by walking together untethered.

The bottom line is that collars and leashes are facts of life for most canines and their people. But these ties don't need to bind. Here, you find out how to choose the right collar and leash for your dog. You also discover how to use that collar and leash correctly so that your walks make both of you happy — but also keep both of you safe.

Types of Collars

When it comes to dogs, a collar isn't just a collar; you have lots of doggie neckwear to choose from. And making the right choice is important, because if you don't, you could injure or even lose your dog. The following list gives you a quick summary of the most common canine neck gear. Table 5-1 also gives you a quick look at how the collars compare to each other.

✔ **Leather collars:** These rolled collars look like leather rings designed for gigantic fingers. Generally, they buckle around the dog's neck. Leather neck gear have several advantages, including the fact that they look nice, smell nice (if you like the smell of leather), and don't damage the dog's fur. However, they often cost more than other types of collars and may not provide the control you need if your pooch is an unruly walker. Leather collars are generally good for puppies, small adult dogs, sensitive pooches, and any other adult dog who's learned to walk nicely on a leash.

✔ **Fabric collars:** Collars made from fabric such as cotton or nylon resemble very small belts or very large watchbands. Some buckle around the dog's neck; others are secured with plastic snap-in clips. Either way, they're suited to well-behaved adult canine walkers, as well as puppies and other small pooches. Fabric collars generally cost less than their leather counterparts do. However, they may be less comfortable for the dog, because they're usually wider than leather collars and touch a larger circumference of the dog's neck.

✔ **Slip collars:** Also known as training collars or choke collars, slip collars were once a mainstay for professional dog trainers as well as for many owners. The collar's mechanism allows the owner to correct a dog's behavior by giving the leash a quick snap, followed immediately by a release. This snap-and-release action puts momentary pressure on a dog's neck, which theoretically creates an incentive for the dog to cease his bad behavior. Moreover, if the collar's made of metal (some are made of fabric), the snap-and-release action causes it to jingle. The jingling sound is supposed to warn the dog to stop whatever he's doing.

In recent years, slip collars have lost favor among many experts. They've realized that this collar can damage a dog's windpipe if the snap-and-release action isn't performed correctly — and that happens more often than not. Instead of performing a quick jerk, many owners pull on the collar without releasing it. The prolonged pull causes their dogs to gasp for breath, but often fails to stop the behavior that prompted the owners to pull on the collar the first place.

A metal slip collar can also literally shave the hair off a dog's neck if he has long hair. In addition, the end of the collar can become entangled on the side of a crate or a railing, causing the dog to literally hang himself.

Bottom line: Most owners don't need to use slip collars and should avoid them. I certainly do.

✔ **Prong collars:** If slip collars are bad, prong collars are worse. This neck gear is exactly what the name says it is: a collar with prongs on it that the dog will feel if the owner needs to pull on the leash. Prong collars hurt. And they're cruel. You don't need to inflict pain or be cruel to teach your dog proper walking etiquette, bathroom manners, or anything else. 'Nuff said.

✔ **Head halters:** If slip collars and prong collars are no-no's, even for unruly canines, what can an owner turn to? The answer is the head halter. This handy little nylon device consists of a loop that goes behind the dog's neck and a second loop that encircles the muzzle. When placed on the dog, it looks a lot like a horse bridle. And, not surprisingly, the head halter guides the dog the same way a bridle guides a horse — where the head goes, the body must follow.

Many trainers recommend head halters not only to restrain rambunctious dogs, but also to deal with other problems such as dogs that lunge at other canines and people or who bark a lot while walking. Their only disadvantages are that some dogs find them itchy and a little difficult to get used to. Head halters are sold under several brand names, including the Halti and the Gentle Leader.

✔ **Body harnesses:** For a small puppy or tiny adult dog such as a Maltese or a Yorkshire terrier, a body harness may be much better than a neck collar. These diminutive pooches are especially vulnerable to trachea problems brought about by conventional neck collars. Body harnesses also are good for dogs with back or disk problems, or breeds such as Dachshunds and other long-bodied canines that are prone to such difficulties. The reason: Body harnesses provide support to the back.

Measuring up

Collars range in size from 12 to 22 inches. To determine your dog's collar size, simply wrap a tape measure fairly loosely around his neck. Add two inches to the measurement, and you'll have his size. For example, a dog whose neck measures 12 inches around would wear a 14-inch collar.

Once you buy the collar and put it on your dog, make sure that it's neither too tight nor too loose. Fasten the collar around his neck and then see whether you can slip two fingers under it. If you can slip more than two fingers under the collar, it's too loose. If your fingers don't fit (or if only one does), the collar's too tight.

Table 5-1		Collar Comparisons	
Type	*Pros*	*Cons*	*Best For*
Leather	Look, feel nice Don't hurt fur More comfortable More durable	More expensive Less control	Puppies Small adult dogs Sensitive dogs Mannerly dogs
Fabric	Less expensive Don't hurt fur	Less comfortable Less durable	Puppies Small adult dogs Mannerly dogs
Slip	More control	Difficult to use	Experts only!
		Can shave off fur May strangle dog Can injure windpipe	Unruly dogs
Prong	More control	Painful for dog	None!!!
Head halter	More control More humane	May be itchy	Unruly dogs
Body harness	Supports back No neck pressure	Less control	Small puppies Tiny adult dogs Long-bodied dogs

Types of Leashes

You don't have quite as many leashes to choose from as collars. Still, enough variety is out there to stump the average dog owner. And just like with collars, choosing the right leash is important — for your comfort, your dog's safety, and the safety of other people whom you and he may encounter. Here's what you should consider as you sort through your leashing alternatives. Table 5-2 also helps you compare your leash options.

   ✔ **Leather leash:** I prefer leather leashes to fabric for two reasons: Leather's easier to hold on to, and it lasts a long time. The easier hold comes in handy if your pooch suddenly bolts while you're holding his leash; with leather, you can tighten your hold without getting the rope burn on your hand that can result from using a cotton or nylon leash. However, there is a definite downside to leather leashes: the cost. A leather tether can cost three or four times more than a nylon or cotton leash of the same length.

✔ **Fabric leash:** Fabric leashes (generally cotton or nylon) carry lower price tags than other types of tethers. They also come in lots of colors, so if you want your dog to make a fashion statement, such as matching his collar to his leash, fabric's definitely the way to go. But such leashes carry significant disadvantages: They're less durable than leather, for one thing. They also feel slippery in the palm of the hand, making them more difficult to grip than leather. And if your dog bolts, pulling the leash across your palm, you may end up with a nasty rope burn. Some manufacturers have tried to make fabric leashes more comfortable by adding extra padding to the handles.

✔ **Retractable leash:** A retractable leash contains a long wire (up to 16 feet) and a hook. The wire resides within plastic housing and can be retracted by pressing a button or lever on the housing. Retractable leashes can extend much further than standard six-foot conventional leashes and probably give your dog a feeling of greater freedom.

But retractables carry several disadvantages. If your dog tends to pull on his leash when he walks, a retractable leash won't help you control him. In fact, some trainers believe a retractable leash encourages such a dog to pull even harder. Another problem with these leashes is that they can be difficult for other people to see. More than once, I've nearly broken my neck when I've tripped over such a leash. Finally, those extra-long lengths are illegal in many communities; for example, New York City prohibits the use of leashes more than six feet long.

These disadvantages don't mean you have to bypass retractable leashes. Just don't use them in populated areas where people can trip over them. Don't use them near streets either; your dog can run into the street and become instant road kill while still attached to the leash.

Table 5-2	Looking at Leashes	
Type	_Pros_	_Cons_
Fabric	Less expensive	Slippery feel
	More lengths to choose	Can cause rope burn
		Not as durable
Leather	Easier to grip	More expensive
Retractable	Longer length	Less control
	More freedom for dog	Harder to grip
		Danger to bystanders

The long and short of leashes

Leashes come in lots of lengths, starting from four feet and stretching to as long as 50 feet. For just walking Fido, though, your best bet is to stick with a six-foot leather or fabric tether. If you opt for a retractable leash, make sure that you don't allow the leash to go much beyond six feet when you and Fido are in crowds or in public places.

Keep in mind that just because you're into leather for your dog's collar, you don't necessarily have to opt for leather with your dog's leash, or vice versa. The same principle (or lack thereof) also is true with fabric. If a leather collar and fabric leash work for you and Fido, that's fine. It's just as fine to choose a fabric collar and leather leash.

And when it comes to leashes, your dog's size doesn't matter. A six-foot leash works just as well with a petite little Chihuahua as it does with a gigantic Great Dane.

Dog-Walking 101

After you've got a collar and leash, you're ready to start walking your pooch. However, taking that first jaunt often involves more than simply putting on the collar on your dog, snapping on the leash, and heading out the door. Before you even open that door, you need to get yourself and your pooch ready. And once you're out the door, you need to make sure that your dog displays at least a modicum of good walking manners.

Good walking manners don't mean that you and Fido must walk together in a simultaneous goose-step, with Fido glued to your left side. That looks elegant in obedience competitions, but can be a pain the neck (especially for the dog) to aim for in real life. It's better instead to aim for an easy stroll in which you're holding the leash loosely, and your dog ambles along. He can be ahead of you, behind you, or beside you — as long as he's not pulling on the leash, and neither of you gets in the way of the other.

Here's how to achieve this pleasurable state of walking affairs:

1. **Do some prep work.**

   A puppy who's never seen, much less worn, a collar and leash before is not likely to saunter off on a walk with you the first time he dons them. He needs time to get used to the feel of the collar and leash first.

Start by buckling or snapping the collar around your canine young-ster's neck. If he doesn't paw at the collar, try attaching the leash. Then, just let him walk around, dragging the leash behind him.

If he accepts the leash and collar and walks around with them easily, take the next step: Pick up the leash very lightly and let him continue to walk. Don't pull on the leash at all; just hold it. Once you're sure he's comfortable, you can begin teaching him in earnest to walk while leashed.

2. Get a grip.

But before you plan on going anywhere, make sure that you've got a proper grip on the leash. If you're using a leather or fabric leash, place the loop around your wrist. Allow the leash to fall across your hand. Then, with the looped hand, grasp the leash just below the loop. With the opposite hand, take hold of the leash between a third and halfway down.

With a retractable leash, of course, the preceding instructions don't apply. Just make sure that you have a firm grip on the plastic handle. And don't use your opposite hand to hold the leash wire; the wire will be slippery and painful to handle.

3. Position the dog.

Once you've got a proper grip on the leash, make sure that your dog's position is equally proper. He should stand next to you on the side opposite your leash-looped hand, and the leash should fall diagonally across your body (see Figure 5-1).

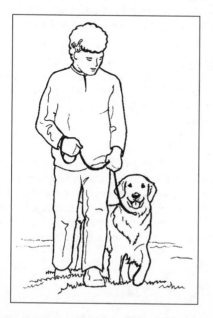

Figure 5-1: A person walking a dog correctly.

It doesn't matter which wrist you use to loop the leash, or which side your dog is placed on. Most professional trainers place dogs on their left-hand sides and loop the leashes around their right wrists — and if asked why, each trainer probably will give you her own individual reason. Bottom line: Don't worry about it. Do what feels best for you.

4. **Get moving.**

   Now you and Fido are ready to start walking. Tell him, "Let's go!" or something equally decisive in a happy, cheerful voice and start moving. Don't jerk on the leash. Chances are, if you've introduced Fido to the leash properly, he'll start trotting along with you. If he doesn't, go back to Step 1 and make sure that he's accustomed to the collar and leash.

5. **Be chatty.**

   When you walk with a two-legged friend, do you saunter in silence? Of course not. So why should that be the case with your four-legged friend? Chat with him as the two of you traverse your neighborhood. A high-pitched, happy-sounding tone of voice will help your dog to focus on you instead of that pesky squirrel scampering around in the yard next door or the garbage truck lumbering down the street. Plus, you'll feel a lot more cheerful.

6. **Keep up the pace.**

   While both of you are learning to use the leash to walk together, it's better to move briskly. Why? A snappy saunter is more likely than a snail's pace to keep your dog's attention focused on you. And if he's focused on you, there's less of a chance that he'll try to range too far afield and ruin the walk for both of you.

   Do keep in mind, though, that a slow pace for people may be a brisk pace for puppies and even some adult dogs. For example, a short-legged Dachshund needs to take at least two or three steps to travel the same ground that a person covers in one easy stride. Make sure that the pace that's reasonably fast for you isn't unreasonably fast for your dog.

7. **Double up on stops.**

   When you stop moving, your dog should stop moving, too. By doing so, your dog won't dart out into traffic when you're stopped at a corner and won't keep moving when you've stopped to tie your shoe. A good way to teach this important lesson to even the youngest puppy is to remove your unlooped hand from the leash and place it in front of his face as you come to a stop.

Dogs with Walking Issues

Many dogs need a little time to master the art of basic leash walking. Some, alas, take longer than others; they have difficulty accepting the very idea of walking while tethered to one of their humans. Here are some profiles of dogs with walking issues and suggestions on how to help them.

The Walk-O-Maniac

Also known as The Dog Who Loves Walking Too Much, this passionate pooch whips herself up into a frenzy of joy and anticipation whenever she sees her owner pick up the leash. The frenzy — which may include frantic yips, high-speed wiggling, or even racing around the room — can make attaching the leash a challenge, and exhaust the dog's human before the walk even starts.

If your dog fits this profile, you need to help her calm down. One way to do so is to simply wait her out. Sit or stand still and remain quiet until your Walk-O-Maniac settles down. Only then should you snap on her leash.

The Walk-O-Phobe

This dog is opposite of the Walk-O-Maniac (see preceding section); he hates anything having to do with the collar and leash. The sight of his owner picking up the leash may send him scurrying off to the farthest corner of the house. Or, if he does permit his owner to attach the leash to his collar, he plants his butt firmly to the ground and keeps it there.

Your walk-o-phobic canine needs you to pretend that he's never seen, much less used, a collar and leash before. Re-introduce him to the collar and leash and make the reintroduction extra gentle. Use a high-pitched, happy-sounding tone of voice to encourage Fido to come to you with the leash attached to him, but without you holding it. Once he readily follows you around with the leash attached, try picking the leash up for a split second. If he doesn't balk, gradually increase the length of time you hold the leash. Once you pass the 30-second mark, try walking.

If Fido starts fighting you at any point in this process, don't fight back. Just go back a step or two and rebuild his confidence. Eventually, he will let you walk him on the leash. He may even turn into a Walk-o-Maniac!

The Sled Dog Wannabe

Many dogs react to the collar and leash by acting as though they're in training for the famous Iditarod sled dog race. They pull as hard as they can and run far ahead of their owners. The owners must hold tightly to the looped ends of the leashes and pray they don't fall flat on their faces.

If this describes your dog's walking style, you need to face facts: Your dog has dethroned you as the leader of your pack, at least while the two of you are out walking. The solution is simple: Regain control of the walk.

Start by letting dog run ahead — at first. When he's stretched the leash taut, do one of two things: Come to a dead stop or turn around and walk in the opposite direction. If you opt to stop, don't start moving again until your dog comes back to you. If you turn around, do so gently; you don't want to jerk your dog or cause him to lose his footing. Either way, your abrupt change of pace will be an unwelcome surprise for your dog. It won't take her long to realize that walks will be much more comfortable and predictable if she focuses her attention on the pace you're setting. In short order, she'll learn to follow your lead. When she does, give her a treat and praise her lavishly.

If you're still having trouble, switch your dog from a conventional collar to a head halter. Then, if your dog goes into Iditarod mode, turn around — but not too quickly, you don't want to jerk her — and walk in the opposite direction. She'll quickly realize that she needs to stay close to you if she wants to maintain her balance.

The Squirrel Hunter

Other dogs walk nicely on the leash until they catch sight of a certain type of fluffy-tailed animal. Then they morph into mighty Squirrel Hunters, hauling themselves and their surprised owners down the street in a frenzied effort to overtake their quarry. The quarry, of course, nimbly scampers up the nearest tree. (It should be noted that other critters — for example, chipmunks, cats, and crows — also can trigger such reactions in otherwise mild-mannered canines. So can cars.)

This scene probably looks pretty funny to a bystander. But for the unfortunate dog walker, a stroll with a Squirrel Hunter can be dangerous, particularly if the walk is taking place on a rain-deluged street or an icy sidewalk. Anyone who's scraped her knees, sprained her ankle, or even just ruined a pair of pantyhose as a result of a Squirrel Hunter's single-minded pursuit understands that this behavior is not desirable.

Anyone who walks a Squirrel Hunter needs, above all, to pay attention. You have to spot that squirrel or other critter *before* your dog does. And once you do catch sight of the squirrel, you must pre-empt your gentle pooch's transformation into fierce hunter.

You can do this in two ways. One is to simply turn around and walk the other way. The second is to slide your unlooped hand further down the leash so that instead of having six feet of leash for your dog to extend, he has only one or two feet. That way, your dog will realize instantly that no matter how many critters he sees, he can't get very far — and chances are, he won't even try. With either solution, you've diverted your dog's attention, and you can continue to walk in peace.

The Laggard

Unlike the Walk-O-Phobe, this dog will go for walks with you. But oh, he is sooooooo slow. He moves along at tortoise-speed when you'd like to pick up the pace a little. Walking around the block with him takes an hour, whereas when you're by yourself it takes all of 15 minutes.

Your Laggard may be just tired; for example, has he just finished up a rousing game of fetch? Is the weather very hot? In such cases, your best bet is to accommodate him: Don't force him to walk. End the walk quickly and let him chill for awhile.

However, a dog who lags behind no matter what may be trying to tell you that he doesn't feel well. For example, the most common symptom of two fairly widespread canine illnesses — arthritis and hypothyroidism — is lagging while walking. For that reason, it's a good idea to bring a habitual Laggard to your vet for a checkup.

But if it's not hot and your vet says he's fine but your dog still makes like Mr. Tortoise to your Mr. Hare, perhaps he's just bored. Try livening things up a little. Go around the block in the opposite direction. Take a different walking route altogether. And vary the pace of your walk a little bit; walk slow some of the time, but fast the rest. Finally, talk to your dog while walking with him: Be animated, happy, and upbeat. You may be surprised at how animated he can be, too.

The Social Butterfly

Some dogs want to spend their walks greeting every canine, feline, and human resident of their neighborhoods. As soon as they see any and all such individuals, they'll pull on their leashes, make like Sled Dog Wannabes or Squirrel Hunters, and race toward that individual. You, meanwhile, are holding on to the other end of the leash and desperately trying to stay on your feet.

Owners of canine Social Butterflies need to be just as vigilant on their walks as owners of Sled Dog Wannabes and Squirrel Hunters must be. Keep on the lookout for creatures your canine extrovert wants to greet. If one strays onto your radar screen, slide your hand down the leash to shorten the length and keep walking. You can also turn around and walk the other way — although if the individual you're walking away from is a person you know, he may wonder why you're doing so!

The Introvert

On the other hand, you may be the human companion of a shy little canine who wants nothing to do with the other residents of your neighborhood. When forced to deal with them, this sort of dog reacts by scurrying behind her owner. In doing so, she manages to entangle both of you in her leash so that starting on your way after the encounter can be difficult (not to mention hazardous) for you both.

Helping your Introvert requires that you employ both short- and long-term tactics. Over the short term, use your unlooped hand to keep the leash short enough to prevent your dog from tangling the two of you up. Over the long term, though, you need to socialize your Introvert — to get her used to the world and help her feel more comfortable in it.

Start by just sitting on your front porch with your Introvert and watch the world go by. Once she's comfortable doing that, stroll up and down your driveway. Beyond that, graduate to walking back and forth in front of your house and then around the block. As your dog becomes more and more comfortable with excursions that take her ever further afield, she can graduate to accompanying you to increasingly crowded places. If you take it slow, her shyness and the leash-tangling should soon be things of the past.

The Anti-Socialist

When I say Anti-Socialist, I'm not talking politics here; I'm talking about dogs who are hostile to one or more other canines. These dogs may express their hostility by barking incessantly, growling, or even lunging at the objects of their hatred.

Even the most mild-mannered dog may feel himself going postal whenever he encounters one particular dog. Just like people, dogs have their own individual likes and dislikes, and it's unreasonable to expect them to like everyone they meet. For example, my Sheltie, Cory, goes into a barking frenzy whenever he sees a particular Maltese in our neighborhood. The reason for his apparent antipathy may be rooted in the fact that the first time they encountered each other, the Maltese tried to bite him.

But whether your dog has issues with just one other canine or is an equal opportunity Anti-Socialist, you need to keep him away from those dogs who don't bring out his better side. If you're walking your leashed dog and you see a pooch whom yours doesn't like, take the easy way out: Cross to the opposite side of the street or turn around and walk in the opposite direction. In fact, it's probably a good idea to play it safe whenever you see a dog you don't know while on your daily jaunts.

The Balker

Sometimes even the most well-mannered canine walker may stop dead in his tracks for no apparent reason. No matter how much you pull, neither the feet nor the rest of the dog budges.

The Balker needs gentle persuasion, not forcible yanking. That's because in all likelihood, this dog is balking because he's seen something that he doesn't understand or that frightens him. Among the more common prompts of canine balking are dumpsters and trash cans — especially at night, when they look big and dark — lawn sculptures, and Halloween decorations (especially those tree-hanging skeletons).

To get your Balker moving again, show that you can protect him from whatever's spooking him. Move ahead of your dog and put yourself between him and the scary object. In a happy tone of voice, encourage your dog to pass the object and come to you. Keep talking until your dog passes the object and reaches you. Then, give him a treat and tell him what a brave boy he is!

Chapter 6

Cleanup Equipment

• •

In This Chapter

▶ Doing the right thing

▶ Curbing versus cleaning up

▶ Choosing an outdoor cleanup method

▶ Using an indoor cleaner

▶ Discovering new cleaning aids

• •

1 never thought much about cleaning up after a dog until I visited Paris.

The City of Lights is also a city of dog lovers. The canine citizens of Paris are even allowed in restaurants — and I'm not talking about just sitting in an outdoor café with Fideau tied to a nearby fence. No, *les chiens de Paris* may venture *inside* their local bistros, where they are welcomed with open arms and plenty of treats.

I loved seeing dogs in bistros, banks, and everywhere else in Paris. And I was thrilled with being able to converse with Parisians about their pooches. But there was one thing about Paris that I totally detested: the dog poop.

Just as dogs were everywhere in Paris, so were their droppings. On the very same day that I discovered how much Parisians love their pooches, I also discovered that Parisians apparently did not believe in cleaning up after those pooches.

Consequently, I found that walking on a Parisian sidewalk was like walking in a minefield. Piles of puppy poop were everywhere: right smack in the middle of the sidewalk, anywhere and everywhere on the street, gracing the tops of the Metro (subway) stairs and tucked discreetly into little corners or next to doorsteps. The life of my shoes depended, literally, on continuously watching where I stepped.

I was, to put it mildly, grossed out. And I was appalled that the residents of such a beautiful city could allow their sidewalks to become so steeped in dog doo.

In recent years, the Parisian city government has taken steps to reduce the local poopload. According to the quarterly *The Bark*, the Parisian municipal government has hired special educators who teach people why they should clean up after their dogs. The city also spends millions of dollars each year to do the cleaning up that the citizens won't.

But the Parisians aren't the only people with dog poop problems. Cleaning up after canines has become a big issue here in the United States, too.

Curbing Versus Cleaning

Americans haven't always been so concerned about cleaning up after their canine companions. Until fairly recently, people have let their doggies do their thing, and then left the doo on the streets and sidewalks.

A few conscientious souls did take the time to curb their dogs. In doing so, they were following the advice of experts. A dog-eared dog care book in my own childhood home (this would have been in the 1960s) exhorted readers to curb their dogs when taking them for walks.

But what exactly is *curbing?*

Curbing is the polite term for a canine waste disposal method that really should be called the Shove-It-Into-The-Sewer approach. A curbed dog is one who's been taught to poop in the street, right by the curb, so that the next rainstorm can sweep his deposits into the nearest gutter. Once in the gutter, the poop and lots of other waste wind their way through a city's sewer system and, eventually, into nearby creeks, streams, and rivers.

Those final destinations — the streams, creeks, and rivers — are one reason curbing is a questionable canine waste disposal method.

Scientists have discovered that dog poop is a major cause of water pollution, and that such pollution poses a significant hazard to human health. In fact, the U.S. Environmental Protection Agency says pet waste is a significant cause of water body contamination in areas where there are high concentrations of dogs.

Canine waste contains lots of nasty bacteria with almost unpronounceable names: fecal streptococcus and fecal coliforms are just two examples. In sufficiently high amounts, these bacteria can make people sick — sometimes very sick. For example, *E. coli* bacteria often causes gastrointestinal infections, as well as infections to the ear, eye, and throat. Another bacteria, campylobacter, can cause diarrhea in humans. Still another form of poop-loving bacteria, salmonella, can cause infections that trigger fever, muscle aches, headache, vomiting, and diarrhea.

And that's not all. According to the University of Maryland's Cooperative Extension Service, dog waste also contains other not-so-lovely disease-transmitting organisms such as roundworms. These parasites can cause their human victims to lose their vision temporarily, as well as trigger coughs and fevers.

Never thought your dog's doo could do so much damage, did you?

And even if dog poop didn't jeopardize human health, there's the matter of whether curbing jeopardizes a dog's safety. I'm not keen on forcing my dog to do his business in the street, where he'd be dangerously close to fast-moving cars, buses, and trucks. A careless driver or spooked dog could easily trigger a traffic accident that would seriously injure or even kill not only the dog, but also human bystanders, passengers, and drivers.

Any way you look at it, curbing is a concept whose time has come and gone. These days, direct cleanup is the way to go.

When you clean up your dog's waste, you don't just shove it somewhere with the idea that Mother Nature will finish the job later. Instead, you physically remove the waste and dispose of it — either through your own household disposal system or by putting it in the trash. Either way, you do what's necessary to prevent the poop from causing discomfort and harm to other people and animals.

Countless communities have jumped onto the canine cleanup band-wagon. From New York to San Francisco, American cities and towns have enacted laws that require their citizens to clean up immediately after their dogs poop. Failure to do so can lead to hefty fines for the human offenders.

Choosing an Outdoor Cleanup Method

What's the best way to clean up your dog's poop? I can think of several criteria that can help you measure a cleanup method's effectiveness.

- ✔ **The ewwwwww factor.** Let's be honest. As much as you love your dog, that love does not extend to his poop. Dog doo is disgusting. That's why people don't want to step in it, and it's undoubtedly why dog owners don't want to have to clean it up. You'd rather not have to even look at the stuff, much less handle it. And you certainly do not want it to come into contact with your shoes, your clothing, or your skin. So it stands to reason that the less a method requires you to deal directly with your dog's droppings, the better that method is.

- ✔ **The disposal factor.** While you don't want to deal with the doo, you don't want it lying around either. And you certainly don't want it to be in your local water supply. That's one reason why curbing no longer cuts it. Any cleanup method must completely remove the poop from the environment for that method to be considered effective.

✔ **The simplicity factor.** I don't know about you, but when I walk my dog first thing in the morning — generally before I have my first hit of caffeine — I'm not up for dealing with anything that requires a lot of physical dexterity or mental planning. And that includes canine cleaning up. I need a method that's no fuss, no muss. As far as I'm concerned, the less complicated the disposal method, the better it is.

✔ **The cost factor.** Having to get rid of a dog's poop is disgusting enough. The idea of having to pay a lot of money — either for equipment to do this yourself or to someone else to do it for you — would add insult to injury.

So with those criteria in mind, you can now assess the three most common methods for cleaning up a dog's poop, assuming the dog has done his business outside. Table 6-1 provides an at-a-glance evaluation.

Table 6-1   Outdoor Cleanup Methods at a Glance

Method	Grossness	Ease of Use	Cost	Best For
Bags	Low/moderate	Very easy	None	Dogs who potty while walking, traveling dogs
Scoopers	Low	Awkward	$15–25	Dogs who potty in own yards
Digester	Low	Easy once installed	$50–75	Dogs who potty in own yards

Bagging it

The quickest, easiest way to get rid of a dog's poop is to put it in a plastic bag and either drop the bag in a trash can or flush the bag's contents down a toilet.

You might think that this method would have a high gross-out factor. And it does — if you use the wrong size bag. There's nothing more disgusting than using a teeny-tiny bag to pick up a great big piece of dog poop and having some of that poop end up on your hand instead of in the bag. But that doesn't have to happen. There are two keys to effective bagging: using the right size bag and developing the proper bagging technique.

What about the toilet?

You may wonder whether you should flush dog poop down the toilet since it shouldn't enter the sewer system via your nearby street gutter. (See the section on curbing, earlier in this chapter.) Happily, the answer is yes.

Here's why: Flushed dog poop, along with human waste, is treated at private or municipal wastewater facilities. These facilities remove the poop from the water. The treated water then enters streams and rivers or is further processed so that it can become drinking water. That contrasts with poop that enters a sewer system via the gutter; such waste bypasses the treatment plant. It flows straight to the stream or river, contaminating them and endangering those who would use them.

For all but the tiniest dogs, a sandwich-sized bag or smaller just isn't big enough to pick up poop. It's far better to choose a larger size, such as an empty bread bag or the plastic bag that your morning newspaper was delivered in. Both these types of bags also carry a second advantage: They're oblong, which greatly eases your ability to get the poop into the bag instead of on yourself.

Before you use your bag, though, check to make sure that it doesn't have any holes. Picking up a bunch of dog doo only to have it hit the ground again is a surefire recipe for frustration.

Once you've got a large enough bag, it's easy to gather up the poop. Here's how:

1. **Pull the plastic bag over one hand like a glove.**

   If you're cleaning up while walking your dog, loop the leash around your wrist and pull the bag over the leashed hand.

2. **Pick up the poop with your bagged hand.**

3. **With your other hand, grasp the open end of the bag and pull the bag inside out.**

   The poop will now be inside the bag.

4. **Knot the bag and drop it into the nearest trash can.**

   Or, take the bag inside and flush the contents down the toilet.

Of course, if there's no trash can nearby, you'll need to carry the bagged poop until you find a suitable receptacle. But take heart. Soon not even the thought of having to tote your dog's poop around town will gross you out. It'll just be a fact of life.

Scooping it

If you simply can't bear the idea of handling your dog's poop — even if there's a bag between the poop and your hand — you may want to consider using a pooper-scooper. These devices consist of various long-handled rakes, shovels, and/or spades that enable the owner to scoop up that poop without having to bend down and get close to it.

In addition to being ideal for the squeamish, pooper scoopers are a good choice for owners whose dogs confine their defecating to their own yards. Even though pooper-scooper laws don't apply to dogs who eliminate on their owners' property, it's still a good idea to pick up your dog's doodoo. That way you'll avoid stepping in it while you're gardening, mowing the lawn, or running to catch an errant toddler (and the toddler won't step in it, either). However, scoopers aren't as good as bags for owners whose dogs potty while walking, because the scoopers are relatively cumbersome to carry.

Pooper scoopers generally cost between $15 and $25. They're available at most pet stores, at pet product Web sites, and in pet supply catalogs.

Help! My lawn is dying!

Plastic bags, pooper scoopers, and dog doo digesters do a great job of removing poop from sidewalks and lawns. But they're totally ineffective in dealing with the damage that a dog's urine can do to a carpet of green grass.

Put very simply, canine urine is the equivalent of capital punishment for that grass. The acid in the pee will kill the grass if the dog anoints it often enough.

Of course, keeping your dog off the grass will do the most to preserve that lush green carpet better known as your front lawn. But if that's not an option — or if your dog gets away from you and takes a whiz on your prized turf — there's help at hand, in the form of a nutritional supplement called GrassSaver. According to the manufacturer, by feeding these liver-flavored tablets to your dog, the pH in his urine is neutralized. When the pH is neutralized, the urine can't kill the grass.

Another, more expensive grass saver comes in the form of a self-irrigating bathroom area called the Patio Park Dog Potty. This canine commode disguised as a fire hydrant provides the dog with limited turf a comfortable place to do his business. The Patio Park comes with a white picket fence, a blue background, and that all-important fire hydrant (a great incentive to help male dogs perfect their aim). The manufacturer recommends this product not only for those who want to save their grass, but also for apartment dwellers, senior citizens, mobility-impaired pets and/or people, and anyone who doesn't want to have to walk her dog after dark. Be prepared for sticker shock, though: The Patio Park costs about $150.

Finally, if you happen to catch your dog anointing your turf (or someone else's), watering the area immediately afterward can also help save the grass.

Digesting it

No, no, no, I'm not suggesting that you eat your dog's poop! And I'm not suggesting that you teach your dog to eat his poop, either.

Some dogs, alas, do like to eat their own droppings. If your dog tries to supplement his diet in this manner, check out Chapter 14.

But if you don't want to put your dog's poop in the trash, or if you like the idea of high-tech waste disposal, you may want to acquire a waste digester system. These small-in-ground systems work the same way septic systems do: They liquefy any dog poop deposited there and drain the liquid into the surrounding soil.

The digester system has two parts: the digester unit itself (including the lid), and the digester mix. Here's how to use them:

1. **Find a convenient but out-of-the-way spot in your yard to install the digester.**
2. **Dig a hole that's about 48 inches deep.**
3. **Install the digester and lid in the hole. The lid should be just a little bit above the ground.**
4. **When your dog poops, bring the poop to the digester, remove the lid, and place the poop inside.**
5. **Add some digester mix and some water and replace the lid.**

   The digester will then do its thing.

Digesters are a good option for the same people who go for pooper scoopers: owners whose dogs do most of their pooping in their own yards. In fact, the two methods can be used together: Use the scooper to transport the poop to the digester and use the digester to process the poop. Digesters can be found at pet stores, in pet supply catalogs, and on pet retail Web sites. The cost, including both the digester unit and the digester mix, ranges between $50 and $75.

Indoor Cleaners

Until your dog is fully housetrained — and perhaps even thereafter, if he becomes ill — he's going to make some mistakes. Instead of doing his business outside, or on the papers or in the litter pan, he'll do it inside: on the floor, on the carpet, on the furniture, on the dinner table, or even on your bed.

Can you recycle it?

Well, yes and no. It's not a good idea to add dog poop to your backyard compost pile. The reason: The compost pile can't get hot enough to kill the disease-causing bacteria that's in the poop.

But according to the University of Maryland's Cooperative Extension Service, there *is* a safe and effective way to recycle dog doo. Just dig a hole or trench that's about five inches deep and bury the poop in it. Microorganisms in the top layer of the soil will break down the poop and release its nutrients into the soil, providing a nutritious meal to nearby plants.

Make sure the hole is away from vegetable gardens or water supplies so that they aren't contaminated by the buried poop.

If your housetrained pooch suddenly starts having bathroom accidents, she could be sick. To find out more about doggie ailments that disguise themselves as potty problems, check out Chapter 15.

In any case, you'll want to get rid of the mess, if only to preserve the surface on which your dog has made his unwelcome deposit. But there's another, more important reason to get rid of the puddle or pile right away, or as soon as possible after you see it.

Canine pee or poop is like a magnet to dogs. If Fido urinates on the carpet and that urine is not cleaned up promptly and thoroughly, Fido will come back to that spot again and again. And, trust me, he will pee on it. To prevent that, you need to not only remove the pee or pile and the stain it leaves in its wake. You also need to remove any odor.

Certain cleaners accomplish all those objectives. Others don't fare so well. Here are some guidelines to finding an effective indoor cleaner:

✓ **Use the right product.** If you're looking for a product that cleans up your dog's bathroom booboos, make sure that the label specifically says that's what the product will do. Why? Because such products contain special enzymes that break down the dog's waste and neutralize its odor. When the odor is neutralized, the dog won't be able to smell the scene of his crime — and, consequently, he won't have any incentive to embark on a repeat performance.

You can find commercial pet stain removal products at any good pet supply store, in pet product catalogs or at most pet supply Web sites. Look for brands such as Natures' Miracle or Simple Solution. Then, be sure to follow the manufacturers' directions.

✔ **Don't use ammonia.** If you use an ammonia-based cleaner to mop up your dog's accident, you can be sure that she will soon return to re-anoint the scene of her crime. That's because ammonia smells like urine to dogs. Consequently, the odor from an ammonia cleaner will draw your pooch back to where she peed before and will prompt her to engage in a repeat performance.

✔ **Forget about club soda.** Some dog owners advocate using club soda in a pinch to clean up a dog's bathroom booboo. While it's true that club soda is cheaper and more readily available than a commercial pet stain remover, the soda is much less effective than the commercial product. Club soda may help remove the stain caused by a dog's bathroom accident, but it does nothing to remove the odor.

Other Cleaning Aids

The products I've described in the preceding sections will more than do the job of cleaning up your dog's bathroom byproducts indoors and out. However, you may also want to consider using a couple of other products and services:

✔ **A black light.** If you think you've removed all traces of stain and odor from your favorite area rug but Fido's still trying to take a whiz on it, consider plunking down $20 or so for a black light. This handy little device locates and illuminates old urine stains that you may not have been able to see. Your indoor pet stain cleaner should be able remove such stains once and for all, although one application may not be enough to do the job.

✔ **A pooper scooper service.** Does the very thought of dealing with your dog's poop — even with a pooper scooper — give you the willies? Are you unable to clean up your dog's poop-sicles because you're a senior citizen or otherwise have difficulty moving around? Or do you just not have the time to deal with cleaning up your poop-laden yard? If so, you may want to consider hiring a professional poop-scooping company. These companies are operating all over the United States and will scoop up your dog's droppings for a surprisingly low cost. For example, in my local area (northern Virginia), a service called Doody Calls (love the name!) will clean your yard weekly for just $12 (2000 rate) per visit.

✔ **Undergarments.** Sometimes even the most trustworthy dog has health problems that temporarily make it impossible for her to hold her water. Until you and your veterinarian figure out why she's having such problems, you can protect your carpets and furniture by fitting your pooch with an undergarment such as a doggie diaper, underpants, or even the canine equivalent of a sanitary napkin. I have more about these garments in the next chapter.

Save that poop!

As strange as it may seem, there will be times in your dog's life when you won't want to get rid of his poop. The most likely occasion for saving the poop is when your vet needs a sample. That's because a sample of your dog's poop, or stool, can tell your vet a lot about your dog's health.

Collecting a usable stool sample is simple: Just place the poop in an airtight container (a clean used margarine tub is great) and bring it to your vet. Keep two things in mind, though:

✔ **Don't load up.** You don't need to ply your vet with your pup's entire fecal output. A teaspoonful or so is more than enough for a vet or lab technician to smear on a microscope slide and see what's going on.

✔ **Get it fresh.** The older the poop, the less revealing it is. Vets generally prefer to see a stool sample that is no more than 12 hours old. If refrigerated, it can be used for up to 48 hours. (But then, do you really *want* to refrigerate your dog's poop?)

Chapter 7

Miscellaneous Gear

. . . .

. . . .

1 thought I'd seen just about every housetraining aid imaginable, until I bought some new vacuum cleaner bags last year.

At the store where I buy my bags is a Labrador Retriever named Abby whose self-appointed mission is to meet and greet customers. During this particular visit, though, Abby wasn't alone. She was getting some help from two tiny Miniature Poodle puppies.

The puppies were adorable and clearly enjoyed helping Abby perform her customer outreach duties. But I was surprised to see such young pooches moving freely around the shop. They didn't look old enough to control their bladders and bowel movements. However, I didn't see any telltale spots on the carpet, nor did I see any newspapers or litter-boxes on the floor.

Since I'm a nosy neighborhood dog lady, I wasn't shy about asking the store owner how he was housetraining the puppies. He obligingly took me to the hallway between the showroom floor and the office. There, spread upon the floor, were several sheets of material that looked a lot like disposable diapers. Atop one of the sheets was unmistakable evidence that the puppies were using the sheets precisely as the store owner had intended.

The sheets were puppy training pads, and that was the first time I saw such pads in action. It was then that I realized that there's a lot more housetraining gear available than I'd ever imagined. However, not all of this gear is necessary. In this chapter, I look at some of the more novel housetraining aids on the market and help you decide when and if you really need them.

The Inside Story

Indoor housetraining items can either help you train your dog to poop and pee in designated places inside your house or provide assistance as you teach your dog to do his business outdoors. The following sections describe the more common indoor housetraining aids.

Puppy training pads

Puppy training pads are an alternative to newspapers or litterboxes for dogs who are learning to potty indoors. The pads are made of absorbent layers of paper, backed by a layer of plastic, and are sealed around the edges. The standard size of each pad is 23 by 24 inches, although at least one manufacturer also offers an "oversize" pad of 30 by 30 inches. The pads come in packages ranging from 12 to 60 pads each.

According to the manufacturers, pads offer three advantages over newspapers: They're better looking, create less mess, and can help dogs learn to potty more quickly. They're also a little cheaper than dog litter.

Because the pads are absorbent, a puppy puddle is less likely to soak through the floor than is the case with layers of newspaper, and cleanup is easier, too. But manufacturers don't stop at trying to make the pads more attractive to dog owners: They want to attract the dogs, too. To do that, manufacturers treat these pads with a special scent — none will say exactly what that scent is — designed to encourage dogs to come to the pad and do their business on top of it.

What about doggie diapers?

Yes, you can get diapers for your dog — but they're not a good idea for housetraining.

A doggie diaper works against a healthy dog's instinctive desire to keep herself and her den clean. It does nothing to teach a dog to "hold it" until she reaches the place where she's supposed to do her business.

But if, for some reason, your housetrained dog can no longer "hold it," doggie diapers can be a big help. For example, older dogs who have lost the ability to control their bladders may do very well with a doggie diaper. So, too, may a dog who has lost the use of her back legs. And for female dogs in season (also known as being in heat), doggie diapers are the canine world's equivalent of maxi-pads.

Still, diapers aren't necessary for healthy canines-in-housetraining. Instead of spending dollars on diapers, it's far better to spend a little time teaching your dog where and when she can go potty.

Prices for puppy training pads range from about $6 to $26, depending on the number of pads in the package.

Baby gates

Baby gates are one housetraining aid that's sold not only in pet stores but also in retail outlets targeted to the parents of human babies and toddlers. Either way, the reasons for using these gates are similar: to erect a barrier that keeps a little one away from danger or out of trouble. For canine children, gates supplement or substitute for crates by confining pooches to permissible areas of the house and preventing them from entering areas where owners don't want them to potty.

 However, not all baby gates are created equal. The U.S. Consumer Product Safety Commission (CPSC) has warned that accordion-style gates pose a serious strangulation hazard to young children. Babies and toddlers have died when they tried to crawl through or over the gates and their heads became entrapped in the V-shaped openings at the top of the gates or the diamond-shaped slats below. It stands to reason that if human children can get their heads caught in these gates, canine children can, too. For that reason, they should be avoided — no matter how cheap the asking prices are at the thrift stores or yard sales where such gates are still sometimes sold. (They haven't been offered at retail stores since the mid-1980s.)

The CPSC suggests that parents choose a gate with a straight top edge and either rigid bars or a mesh screen. For a puppy, I'd go a little further and recommend that any bar gate be covered with mesh; the mesh will eliminate any chance of a puppy's head becoming entrapped between the bars.

 And speaking of entrapment, be careful when you install the gate. Make sure that the bottom of the gate is close enough to the floor to prevent a determined puppy from slipping underneath it and making an escape — or worse, getting stuck.

Aside from safety considerations, your major quandary when purchasing a baby gate for your puppy is deciding between a pressure-mounted gate and a hardware gate. The former type relies on pressure to ensure that the gate adheres to the walls. Pressure gates are easier to install than a gate that requires hardware, but they're also easier for rambunctious puppies to knock down than hardware gates are.

If you do opt for a pressure-mounted gate, consider whether you want one that swings open or one that you need to hop over. The latter is cheaper than the former, but hopping over that gate gets old very quickly — especially if you trip over the gate and fall flat on your face. Almost all hardware gates swing open; that's another factor in their favor.

Don't bother with this item

One thing you don't need is a "housebreaking aid." This is a polite term for special drops designed to show Fido where you want him to do his business.

Using one of these products may be tempting to the person who's hoping against hope that there's some sort of magic potion that enables one to housetrain a dog instantly. Alas, there is no such product. Your dog won't learn proper potty manners without your help, guidance — and, above all, your time.

Save your money and keep things simple. Don't bother buying a housebreaking aid. Take the time to teach your dog appropriate bathroom behavior.

Finally, before buying any gate, make sure that you measure the width of the doorway where the gate will be installed, and bring those measurements with you to the baby products store or pet store. You should be prepared to part with about $25 for a pressure gate, and as much as $75 for a hardware gate.

Exercise pens

Exercise pens — or x-pens for short — are somewhat similar to children's playpens. And, in fact, their functions are similar: to confine youngsters who haven't yet figured out which places they should and shouldn't go.

X-pens are made from the same sort of metal wire used to manufacture wire crates. In fact, they resemble wire crates, except for the fact that x-pens lack tops and bottoms. Most x-pens have eight panels plus a door. They range in height from 24 to 48 inches, and they cost between $65 and $120.

An x-pen can be a good housetraining alternative for the crate-phobic dog. Be careful, though, to make sure that your dog can't jump over it or knock it over.

More information on housetraining the dog who hates her crate is contained in Chapter 9.

Litter supplies

If you've decided to train your dog to use a litterbox (and if you have, Chapter 9 tells you how to do it), you'll need to stock up on a couple of special items. They are

✔ A litter tray, similar to what cats and kittens use to go to the bathroom. The trays have walls on three sides; the fourth side is open to allow easy entry. One company, Purina, offers three litter pan sizes: one for puppies and dogs who weigh less than six pounds; one for pooches up to 15 pounds; and one for dogs who weigh up to 35 pounds. Prices for pans range from $9 to $19, depending on the size you purchase.

✔ The litter itself. This is the stuff you put into the litter pan. The main ingredients are recycled paper and/or wood pulp. The cost for dog litter ranges between $5 and $10 per bag, depending on the size you buy.

Ins and Outs

There's really just one item that fits into the category of indoor-to-outdoor gear: the doggie door. This canine-sized portal provides a passage between the inside of your house and an outside yard. Covering the passage is a flap or panel that the dog pushes aside with his nose. Thus, as Figure 7-1 shows, a dog with a doggie door can take himself outside whenever he needs a potty break.

Figure 7-1: A doggie door enables your dog to take himself outside whenever he needs to go.

A dog door can be a simple portal-and-flap affair or an elaborate electronic system. Different models are designed to be installed in walls, French doors, or regular doors. Prices start at about $20 for a simple door sized to fit a small dog, while a full bells-and-whistles electronic system can cost as much as $800 for a large dog.

Doggie doors can be a godsend for already-housetrained dogs and their people. With unlimited access to the outdoors, the dog isn't forced to "hold it" all day while you're at work, and you don't have to get up to let Fido out in the middle of the night.

Make sure that the doggie door leads your dog to a secured area: either a fenced back yard or some sort of dog run. Experts also suggest that the door be closed and locked when it's not needed, and that it be installed in an inconspicuous area of your house.

And don't rely on the doggie door until your pooch has mastered his housetraining fundamentals. It's complicated enough for some dogs to figure out where and when to do their business without also having to learn to maneuver that doggie door flap. Bottom line: Housetrain your dog first and *then* teach him to use the doggie door.

For the Great Outdoors

Other housetraining equipment is meant to be used outside. Some is helpful during the actual housetraining process, while other gear listed here is best used only after your pooch has mastered his bathroom basics.

Fencing

A fenced yard can be the foundation of an outdoor paradise for your pooch. It can also make housetraining easier if — and this is a big if — you realize that you are still the one who needs to teach Fido when and where to do his business. That means you need to go out with him while he learns to poop and pee outdoors. Only when he's mastered the art of outdoor bathroom behavior can you stay inside while he heads out into the yard to do his thing.

Still, there are undeniable advantages to having a fenced yard. For one thing, you don't need to hassle with collars and leashes every time Fido needs to make an outdoor pit stop. And in the mornings and evenings, you can stay in your pajamas and bathrobe while you take Fido to his backyard bathroom. That certainly beats having to get dressed and embark on a bleary-eyed walk around the neighborhood with your canine potty trainee.

What about electronic fencing?

Electronic fencing sounds like a dream come true. Manufacturers of these boundary systems claim that they teach your dog to stay within the boundaries of your property without your having to erect a conventional fence. The dog wears a special collar that gives him an electrical shock if he "crosses the line."

However, such fencing is far from foolproof. Some determined canine escape artists venture beyond their property lines despite getting shocked by their collars, only to refuse to come back home because they don't want to endure another shock upon re-entry. Another problem is that other dogs, animals, or people can enter the yard freely, but your dog can't escape from them. That makes him vulnerable to being attacked, poisoned, or stolen.

As with so many other products, electronic fencing seems to promise a shortcut to teaching and taking care of your dog. All too often, though, such shortcuts only shorten the path to problems.

Just make sure that the fencing you install doesn't awaken the escape artist in your dog's soul. Ask your local hardware store and fencing contract professional which materials are best for keeping canines within their own yards. And as you or your contractor install the fence, make certain that there are no openings or crevices — either above ground or underground — that provide portals through which Fido can make an escape.

Finally, don't turn your dog out into the backyard and leave him there all day, every day. Would you want to be in the same place every day, with no way to leave it (and for those of you who are saying, I'm-in-the-same-office-every-day, I say at least *you* can escape to the water cooler)? All too often, yard dogs become bored dogs — and bored dogs frequently turn into noisy dogs who bark all day, or destructive dogs who resort to digging in a desperate attempt to escape the yard or simply amuse themselves. Your neighbors will be grateful if you keep your dog inside with you most of the time. Your yard will look better, too.

Tie-outs

A *tie-out* is a device in which your dog is tethered to either an overhead or in-ground device that has a retractable cable. They're handy devices to have around, particularly if you don't have a fenced yard, but you need to use them with care.

During my childhood, my parents found a novel way to minimize the hassles entailed in taking our already housetrained Dachshund, Casey, out for potty breaks. Atop one of the posts on our front porch was a little device called a Dog Tenda that vaguely resembled a retractable leash. My parents (and later my brother and me, when we were tall enough) would reach up to the Dog Tenda, pull down its retractable cable, and attach the cable to Casey's collar. Then we would come inside, and Casey would race off the porch and into the front yard to do his business. When Casey finished, he'd come running back on to the porch and bark to come inside.

At the time, that seemed like a great system. But I wouldn't use a Dog Tenda or any other tie-out in the same way today. And I certainly wouldn't rely on one to housetrain a dog.

The trouble with tie-outs for housetraining is that they really don't work. If you use one and expect the dog to figure out what to do, you're setting yourself up for disappointment, and you're setting your dog up for frustration. You're really asking your dog to housetrain himself — and even though most dogs are quite intelligent, that particular task is probably beyond their abilities.

When it comes to housetraining, a dog needs his human to show him what to do. Your canine companion probably has all the instincts necessary to make housetraining easy, but he still needs you to guide him. If you rely on a tie-out to teach him the art of outdoor bathroom manners, he's not going to learn what you want him to — at least not very effectively.

And even after your dog is housetrained, using a tie-out for potty breaks isn't wise. The pitfalls here are the same as with electronic fencing: If an unleashed dog or other animal ventures onto your property, the tie-out limits your dog's ability to get away or otherwise defend himself.

Still, tie-outs can be handy under certain circumstances. I use one with my current dog, Cory. I like having him outside in the backyard with me, even though we don't have any sort of fence to keep him there should he decide to stray. So we have a little tie-out — one that's very similar to Casey's old Dog Tenda — attached to one of the planters on our backyard patio. Whenever Cory joins my family and me out back, we attach the tie-out cable to his collar. Thanks to the tie-out, Cory can be with us, and we can enjoy what we're doing without having to worry about his straying out of our yard. However, we never leave Cory alone on the tie-out. When we go back inside, he comes with us.

And that's the key: A tie-out is a good way to ensure your dog's safety outside if you don't have a fenced yard — as long as a responsible person is out there with him.

Chain, chain, cha-yains . . .

Although the use of tie-outs under very limited circumstances is fine, the practice of chaining a dog isn't fine, ever.

Putting a stake in a yard, attaching a chain to the stake, attaching the chain to a dog, and then leaving the dog out in the yard all day is traumatic for the animal. Sure, he's getting some fresh air, and you don't have to worry about taking him out for a potty break. However, he's missing precious time inside with you and the rest of the pack. I can't stress this enough: Dogs are social beings, and they need to be with other dogs and people if they are to be emotionally healthy. Moreover, chaining exposes a dog to danger from free-roaming dogs and other animals. People have begun to realize that chaining a dog is nothing short of abusive. In fact, according to the Washington (D.C.) Humane Society, several cities have outlawed the continual chaining of dogs. Citizens of these cities now understand that while chains may have been great for Aretha Franklin's career, they're terrible for dogs.

Dog runs

If you don't want to fence your entire yard but want a safe outdoor place for your dog to do his business, you may opt for a *dog* or *kennel run*. This small fenced area — say, six to ten feet by six feet — provides a private place in your yard for your pooch to go to the potty. However, just like with fenced yards and doggie doors, dog runs are no substitute for your role in the housetraining process. Moreover, dog runs can be expensive; for example, one company's 6-foot by 6-foot by 6-foot chain-linked dog run costs more than $600.

Clothing

Not very long ago, I thought that dressing a dog in a raincoat and boots was silly — something that only dog lovers with too much money and no human children indulged in. But that was before Cory entered my life. The little guy truly detests getting his paws or fur wet if we have to take a walk in the rain. He frequently makes this antipathy crystal clear by practically Velcro-ing himself to my leg while we take our soggy strolls (the better to benefit at least a little from the protection of my umbrella). Even worse, though, is that during rainy weather he'll often refuse to leave my side to do any peeing or pooping.

I can't attach an umbrella to Cory, but I have begun to wonder if a rain-coat might help him deal with downpours a little better. Fortunately, some enterprising retailers offer some answers to that question in the form of surprisingly stylish canine raincoats. These doggie duds range from a simple slicker that costs less than $10 for a small dog to a patent leather, fully lined raincoat that retails at a whopping $160 for a large pooch.

But there's more to outdoor canine gear than just raincoats. Sweaters, winter coats, and boots offer lots of fashion options for the style-conscious canine. And these garments do more than keep your dog in style; they also keep her warm during winter's icy blasts. In fact, for short-haired dogs, such gear may be a necessity to protect them from the elements. However, even long-haired pooches such as Cory may appreciate having an extra layer between their tresses and the elements.

Boots can help protect any dog's paws from winter salt, ice between the toes, and other weather-induced unpleasantries that make all too many dogs reluctant to potty outdoors.

Of course, it's important to make sure that your dog's new duds fit him properly. And just like for people, canine clothing sizes are fairly well standardized. To figure out your dog's size, first determine his top line measurement by stretching a tape measure between the base of his neck (the place where his neck joins his body) to the base of his tail (the place where his tail starts). Then measure his chest by wrapping the tape measure around his trunk at the widest point, which usually is just behind his front legs. With those measurements in hand, you can determine your dog's clothing size, as shown in Table 7-1.

Table 7-1	Sizing Up		
Size	*Abbreviation*	*Top Line*	*Chest*
Extra small	XS	6 to 9 inches	12 inches
Small	S	10 to 13 inches	14 inches
Medium	M	14 to 17 inches	17 inches
Large	L	18 to 20 inches	20 inches
Extra large	XL	21 to 25 inches	23 inches
Extra-extra large	XXL	26 to 30 inches	25 inches

If your dog's measurement falls between two sizes, or if his chest measurement puts him in a larger size category than his top line measurement does, get him the larger size.

Footgear for your dog may also come in sizes, too. One retailer suggests measuring your dog's paw from the heel to the toe, excluding the toenails. Based on that measurement, Table 7-2 shows you how you can size up canine footwear.

Table 7-2	If the Shoe Fits . . .	
Size	*Abbreviation*	*Measurement*
Extra small	XS	1.25 inches
Small	S	1.75 inches
Medium	M	2.25 inches
Large	L	2.75 inches
Extra large	XL	3.25 inches

Again, if the measurement falls between two sizes, buy the larger one.

Decked out in such finery, your dog will not only look good — he'll also probably feel better, even when the weather outside makes you feel miserable. Chances are, he'll do his job better too, or least he'll do it more quickly.

Part III

Getting Down to the Nitty-Gritty

The 5th Wave   By Rich Tennant

THE **3** Magic Words of Happiness for Doug, His Wife, and Their Dog: Home Sweet Home... I Love You...

...LOW STOOL VOLUME...

DOG CHOW

In this part . . .

*H*ere's where you begin to housetrain your dog in earnest. This part details the three methods — paper training, litter training, and outdoor training — that you can use to teach your dog where and when to do his business. You also discover how to adapt any of these methods to your specific schedule, what to do if Fido has trouble learning his bathroom basics, and when you can consider him to be fully housetrained.

Chapter 8

Indoor Training

*O*nce upon a time, not very long ago, Bartok was a housetraining whiz. The two-year-old Miniature Dachshund had no problem holding his pee and poop all day while his human owners went out to work. In fact, Bart had not only aced his housetraining basics — he'd even learned to eliminate on command.

But when one of Bart's owners departed the household and the other owner began working even longer hours, the little dog's bathroom manners began to backslide. The once-dry Mini Dachshund began leaving puddles all over his house. Bartok's remaining owner, who quickly became frustrated at having to spend her evenings cleaning the carpet, began wondering whether her dog needed a new way to go to the bathroom — and if so, whether indoor training would fill the bill.

The answer to that question could very well be "yes." It's very possible that Bartok simply can't refrain from peeing during the many hours that his owner is at work. The dog may well have been pushing his personal no-peeing limit *before* his owner began working longer hours. When those hours increased, something had to give — and that something was Bart's bladder. Having an indoor bathroom can solve that problem by giving the dog a place to potty indoors whenever he needs to.

In this chapter, I explain why indoor training may be the solution to many pooches' potty problems and describe exactly how to teach your canine companion to use an indoor potty.

When to Consider Indoor Training

If your outdoor-trained dog suddenly starts making bathroom mistakes, it's crucial to have his veterinarian examine him for possible medical problems, some of which can be life threatening. Chapter 15 outlines some of these problems and how to solve them. In any case, though, dealing with housetraining lapses should start with a trip to your vet.

But if your canine companion gets the all-clear from his doctor, switching to indoor training may be a good idea — and not just for home-alone dogs, either. Pooches whose people have trouble walking, dogs who live in city apartments and can't get to an outdoor potty area easily, and/or very small dogs may all do better with indoor potties than with outdoor bathrooms.

For a dog whose owner is away from home all day, moving the canine potty indoors may be a big improvement from cleaning up a puddle when she comes home. For a senior citizen who can't get around easily, an indoor potty may make the difference between being able to have a dog and having to live without canine company. For the high-rise apartment dweller, having an inside place for the dog to do his business is far better than making a mad dash for the elevator to get Fido outside in time. And for anyone with a reasonably small dog, indoor training eliminates the need to brave bad weather when taking the dog outside.

Indoor Training Theory and Practice

Indoor training is, quite simply, the process of teaching your dog to poop and pee only in the indoor potty that you've created for him. The potty generally is either a few layers of newspaper spread out on the floor, or a litterbox tucked discreetly into the corner of a room.

A successfully indoor-trained pooch is one who, upon feeling the urge to eliminate, high-tails it to the papers or the litterbox. Once he's atop the papers or in the box, he does his business. Afterward, you change the litter or the papers.

Indoor training involves using scent and repetition to teach your dog that the litter or the spread-out newspaper is the only surface upon which she should potty. For paper trainees, there's a second part to the process: reducing the amount of floor area covered by the papers, so that doggie bathroom is relatively inconspicuous.

Of course, the devil is in the details. But take heart. You and your dog can master those details quickly and make indoor training a breeze. First, though, you need to decide which type of indoor potty you'll use: newspapers or a litterbox (see the next section).

Newspapers Versus Litterbox?

Choosing between newspapers and a litterbox is a pretty subjective matter. Each has an equal number of advantages and disadvantages, as Table 8-1 shows.

Table 8-1	Papers Versus Litter	
	Pros	*Cons*
Paper	Cheap Convenient	Messy cleanup Messy-looking
Litter	Tidy-looking Easy cleanup	More expensive Less convenient

The first time you clean up a few squares of newspaper soaked in dog pee, the potential messiness of this enterprise will become clear. You'll discover that if you don't pick up the paper carefully, the pee that was on the paper may drip down to the floor — or worse, onto you. Plus, those newspapers never look very nice when they're spread out on your floor, even before your dog uses them.

Litterboxes look much better on the floor than newspapers do. And litterbox cleanup is far less messy than newspaper cleanup is: You just scoop the used litter into the trash and flush any solid waste down the toilet. Baseball great Johnny Bench's remarks about Krylon paint could apply just as well to doggie litterboxes: "No runs, no drips, no errors."

However, newspapers carry one big advantage over litterboxes: They're cheap. In fact, unless you purchase newspapers strictly for use as a puppy potty, they're free. If you're like most people, though, you first use your newspaper to learn what's going on in the world and then let your canine companion do her business on it.

Another plus for newspapers is that they're very convenient — especially if you get them delivered to your home every day. Of course, you also can get dog litter delivered to your home, if you order online or from a catalog. Unlike with newspapers, though, you need to remember to place that order, and you have to pay shipping and handling charges.

Ultimately, the solution to the newspaper versus litter quandary is a matter of personal preference. If you hate the look of newspapers all over your floor, a litterbox may be a good alternative. On the other hand, if you want to housetrain your pooch as cheaply as possible, newspapers have the edge.

Where to Put the Indoor Potty

Over the past few years, many people have become convinced that harmony in the home depends on the way they arrange the furniture in that home. Figuring out just how to do that is the essence of an ancient discipline called Feng Shui.

But while Feng Shui is new to many people, more than a few dog owners may have been practicing it (after a fashion) for a long time. They've discovered that housetraining becomes a lot easier when the dog's living area — his home within your home — is arranged appropriately. This is particularly true when it comes to indoor training. Finding the right place to put your dog's indoor potty makes bathroom breaks go much more smoothly for both you and your canine companion.

Did you notice that I said "home within your home"? I said that for an important reason: Until your dog is fully housetrained, he should not — no way, no how — have access to your entire home unless you can be right there to watch his each and every move.

This no-total-access rule is crucial whether you live in a pocket-sized apartment or an abode that rivals Hearst Castle. That's because if you're not watching what Fido is doing, you're less likely to see when Fido's about to have an accident. You'll have to clean up the accident after the fact — and whenever that happens, you've missed a golden opportunity to remind Fido where he should do his business.

So during those times that you can't pay close attention to your indoor trainee, you need to confine him to a space within your space: a dog-proofed living area that he can call his own. The living area starts with a soft, comfy bed, possibly within a crate. But that's just the beginning; your pooch also needs a place to eat and a place to potty.

Pointers on setting up a pet's feeding area — in particular, tips on choosing dishes — are in Chapter 12.

Once you've got those essentials though, you need to decide where to put them. Here are some factors to consider when figuring out where your puppy's living area should be.

- ✔ **Your dog's needs:** Your indoor trainee needs more than just a place to sleep, eat, poop, and pee. He also needs for that living area to be located in the middle of his household's action.

  Put very simply, your dog needs to feel as though he's part of your family. He needs to see and hear most of what's going on. And he needs to get plenty of attention from every family member. That attention is a whole lot easier to give if the dog is close to where every family member is.

A dog is — first, last and foremost — a social being. The closer he is to his people, the happier he'll be. And you'll be happier, too, because the time your puppy or dog spends in the hub of the household will give him the mental and social stimulation he needs to become an emotionally healthy, easy-to-live-with member of your family.

✔ **Your needs:** When figuring out where to place a dog's living area, the most important consideration for the humans in the family is that the area be easy to clean. That's because no matter how carefully you follow the instructions in this book, your pooch will probably have at least a few accidents before he masters the art of proper potty behavior. It's crucial — for your own peace of mind and for your four-legged friend's housetraining progress — to remove those accidents easily and thoroughly.

It's much easier to whisk away a puddle or pile that's been deposited on a linoleum floor than one that's gracing a living room carpet. The floor accident can be wiped away with paper towels and a commercial pet-stain cleaner, and no one will be the wiser. However, the carpet accident — especially if it's from dog pee — can soak into the carpet and the padding underneath. A commercial cleaner can obliterate the stain and odor, but also can also soak through the carpet to the padding. That means a long drying time. Plus, if the carpet and pad are soaked often enough, they can become lumpy.

For some people, home décor is almost as important as easy cleanup. If you've painstakingly decorated your home to resemble an interior spread from *Architectural Digest*, you'll want to make sure that your puppy's part of your palace doesn't detract from the effect you want to create. And even if your furniture comes from IKEA instead of from Ralph Lauren, you may still want to locate your puppy's palace in the less formal rooms of your home (for example, not in the dining room with the sideboard full of china you inherited from your grandmother).

✔ **Your home layout:** The room in which you establish your dog's space needs to have enough square footage for both you and him to go about the business of living. These criteria may prompt you to place your dog's living area in a different part of your home than someone else might. That's okay. There is no one-size-fits-all best place to locate your puppy's palace.

Many people opt to house their dogs in their kitchens, and that often makes a lot of sense. After all, kitchens often are relatively large, the floors are easy to clean, and families tend to gather there more than just about any other room in the house. However, corralling a dog in the kitchen may not be practical if that room is very small — as is often the case in many city apartments. If that's your situation, consider taking a page from the book of an apartment-dwelling single woman I knew: House your dog in your bedroom with you. For her, that made sense: She watched TV in her bedroom and liked to read there as well. By keeping the dog's living area in her bedroom, the dog got to spend lots of time with her, without her having to watch him every second.

When it comes to litterboxes, it's also nice if the room in which you place the box is close to a covered trash disposal area and to a sink. The trash area is needed for litter disposal; the sink is needed to wash the litterbox.

Once you've decided which room your puppy will share with you, it's time to arrange his things. Generally, there's just one cardinal rule here: Place the bed and dishes away from the designated potty area. For example, if you've placed his bed and dishes at one end of the living area, lay the papers down at the opposite end. By doing this, you'll encourage your dog's instinctive desire to keep his sleeping and dining areas clean.

Make sure, too, that your puppy can't get into any trouble inside or outside his living area. Install baby gates to block the doorways, or encircle the living area with an exercise pen. Within the living area, remove any dangling electrical cords from the dog's reach, and make sure he can't get into any cabinets where cleaners and other hazardous substances are kept.

Door guards, which are sold in the baby departments of toy stores, can keep your curious canine from venturing into your cabinets.

Now you're ready to place the indoor potty in the living area. If you're using a litterbox, place it in a corner away from your puppy's bed and dishes. If you're using newspapers, take several two-page foldouts of newspaper and spread them out on the floor, one on top of the other. When your dog is first learning to potty properly, you may want to cover all but a small strip of the entire living area with newspaper. Then, as he begins to show that he knows where to go, you can gradually reduce the papered-over area.

Paper pointers

Not all papers are created equal, at least when they're being used to create puppy potties. Your everyday newspaper — the one with black print and occasional front-page color photos — is the best possible surface for a dog's bathroom business. Not only is it more absorbent than other surfaces, it also provides more traction. Other surfaces, such as magazines and advertising inserts, are too slippery for many puppies to even stand on, much less squat on. Moreover, they don't absorb a puppy's puddles; the stuff just stays pooled on top of the paper.

Don't fret if the ink from the newspaper rubs off on your light-coated puppy's paws. A little dab of soap and water will whisk those smudges away.

Put some plastic between the papers and the floor to keep your dog's deposits from soaking through the papers. A plastic shower curtain liner is ideal.

Indoor Training for Puppies

Once you've set up your puppy's living area, you can start teaching her to use the indoor potty. The first and most important step is to help her make the connection between the potty place and what she's supposed to do in that place.

Start off right — and do it right away. Car rides often prompt a puppy to eliminate immediately after the ride is over. So as soon as you and your pup arrive home from the breeder's, take her to the papers or litterbox. When she opens her floodgates and/or makes a solid deposit, praise her lavishly. Let her know that she's done exactly what you wanted her to do.

Then, clean up the papers or litter immediately, but save one of the soiled pieces. Place this soiled layer just below the top layer of fresh newspaper or underneath the litter. By doing so, you're telling your puppy where you want her to do her business. The smell of the soiled paper or litter is the canine equivalent of a come-hither glance.

You know how grossed out you get if you find you have to use a dirty bathroom? Well, your dog feels the same way. Plan on washing the litterbox out with detergent and warm water at least once a week and on freshening the litter each time your dog uses the box. If you're using papers, change the papers as soon as they're soiled (except for that pre-scented piece).

Once she's pottied and you've changed the papers or litter, let your puppy explore the house for awhile. But keep a close eye on her for signs that she needs to go again. If she suddenly stops in the midst of her explorations, starts sniffing intently, begins to circle, and/or starts to squat, whisk her back to the litterbox or papers. Praise her if she pees or poops there. On the other hand, if you miss the signs that she's going to go, and she subsequently misses the papers or box, don't say anything. Just clean up and resolve to watch her more closely next time.

After an hour or so of getting to know each other, put your puppy in her bed and let her take a much-needed nap. Watch to see when she wakes up, though — and when she does, make sure that she gets to the box or papers. If you see her use them, tell her what a good puppy she is. Then, change the papers or litter as before.

You'll find that your puppy will need to head to her indoor potty after every meal, naptime, and play session. Keep an eye on her when she does. Each time she uses her potty, praise her lavishly. When she uses her potty consistently, you won't need to use a soiled layer to lure her there.

If you're using newspapers, consistent use also means you can start reducing the size of the papered area. Leave a little bit more of the floor unprotected each time you change the papers, until you finally have an area that's about the size of four one-page sheets placed together.

Don't take your puppy outside for a walk or to play until she makes a trip to the papers or the box. You don't want the pup to associate the outdoors with elimination. You're aiming to have your puppy consider the papers or litterbox to be her one and only toilet area.

Sometimes, though, indoor training may not be a permanent solution to a dog's potty problems. For example, an apartment dweller with an indoor-trained dog may want to move the canine bathroom outdoors if he purchases a house with a nice big yard. If you're looking to make the indoor-to-outdoor switch, see Chapter 10.

Crates and the Indoor Trainee

If you're planning to indoor-train your puppy, does he really need a crate? After all, you're not trying to teach him to hold his poop and pee until you take him outside, right?

The answer to the second question is no, you're not. And the answer to the first is, no, he doesn't absolutely have to have a crate — but investing in one is still a good idea.

No matter what method you use to housetrain your four-legged friend, he is still a dog. He still retains those canine instincts that harken back to his wild ancestry. One of those instincts is the need to have a safe, enclosed place from which to view the world: a den. A crate gives your dog that secure vantage point.

It's true that indoor-trained dogs don't need to hold their poop and pee for as long as outdoor-trained dogs often do. Still, you probably don't want your dog to be traipsing to the papers or litterbox at any and all hours. By teaching him to stay in his crate for at least fairly short intervals, you're helping him develop the control he needs to put a temporary hold on his deposits.

When to Schedule Bathroom Breaks

Even indoor-trained dogs can benefit from learning to hold their poop and pee. The pooch with some self-control is much easier to live with than the dog with unregulated bathroom demands. It's also easier to determine that your dog may be ill if you can determine whether he's going more or less often than usual; with a dog who potties unpredictably, making such a determination is impossible.

But your dog's bathroom behavior needn't flummox you. You can bring some order to your indoor trainee's life (and your own) by putting his trips to the potty on a schedule.

The important thing to remember when setting up a potty schedule is that puppies need to eliminate at the following times:

- ✔ When they awaken from naps
- ✔ After vigorous playing
- ✔ After eating

Armed with this knowledge, you can create a schedule that gives your puppy enough time to pee or poop, but also gives you some predictability. Table 8-2 shows you how you might structure a schedule for a three-month-old pup.

Table 8-2	Indoor Training Schedule for Three-Month-Old Puppy
Time	*Tasks*
7:00 a.m.	Get up.
	Take puppy to papers or litterbox.
	Put puppy in crate.
7:30 a.m.	Feed puppy.
	Offer water.
	Take puppy to papers or litterbox.
	Play with puppy up to 15 minutes.
	Put puppy in crate.

(continued)

Table 8-2 *(continued)*

Time	Tasks
Midmorning	Offer water.
	Take puppy to papers or litterbox.
	Play with puppy up to 15 minutes.
	Put puppy in crate.
Noon	Feed puppy.
	Offer water.
	Take puppy to papers or litterbox.
	Play with puppy 15 to 30 minutes.
	Put puppy in crate.
Midafternoon	Offer water.
	Take puppy to papers or litterbox.
	Play with puppy up to 15 minutes.
	Put puppy in crate.
5:30 p.m.	Feed puppy.
	Offer water.
	Take puppy to papers or litterbox.
	Play with puppy up to 1 hour and/or let puppy hang out with family in the kitchen.
7:00 p.m.	Take puppy to papers or litterbox.
	Play with puppy up to 15 minutes.
	Put puppy in crate.
Before bed	Take puppy to papers or litterbox.
	Put puppy in crate.
During the night	Take puppy to papers or litterbox if necessary.

As your puppy gets older, she won't need the midmorning, midafternoon, and 7 p.m. trips to the papers, and she won't need the noontime feeding, either. The nocturnal trip to the potty will soon become a thing of the past, too.

Can you use cat litter?

If you've got both a dog and a cat, you may be thinking about streamlining your shopping by purchasing the same litter for both. But according to litter manufacturers, that's not a very good idea.

For one thing, many dogs are under the strange impression that kitty litter is gourmet fare for dogs. Consequently, they're at least as likely to try eating the stuff as they are to eliminate in it. Such behavior can pose problems not only for your canine companion, but also for your feline friend.

And even if your dog figures out what he's supposed to do in the kitty litter, that litter probably won't be up to the job. That's because many cat litters, particularly the clumping kind, are sandlike in texture. Cats like to cover their solid waste, and the sandlike litter makes that coverup action easier. On the other hand, dogs don't cover their tracks — or their poop, either. However, some canines do scuff and scrape the areas behind them with their rear feet after they've made a solid waste deposit. A dog who likes to do this would end up kicking a fair amount of kitty litter out of the box. Dog litters, which are made from recycled paper and/or wood pulp, are much more likely to withstand a dog's rear-guard action.

These differences in feline and canine behavior also mean that household dogs and cats need to have separate litterboxes. If you expect Fido to potty in the same box that Fluffy does — or vice versa — it's likely that both Fido and Fluffy will choose to do their business elsewhere.

More information on when to feed a dog — and what to feed her — is contained in Part IV.

This schedule assumes that someone's home during the day to take care of the puppy's potty needs. If that's not the situation in your home, check out Chapter 10.

Indoor Training for the Adult Dog

If you've just adopted an adult dog who's always pottied indoors, there's really no training to do. Just continue with the routine he's brought with him from his previous home. More often, though, indoor-training an adult dog means moving his bathroom from the outdoors backyard to a location inside your house.

From outdoors to papers

Moving a dog's potty from an outdoor spot to the front page of yesterday's newspaper is relatively easy. Start by bringing a piece of toilet tissue and a piece of newspaper along when you take Fido outdoors to his usual potty place. After he eliminates, use the toilet tissue to bring the deposit into contact with the newspaper.

The next time you take Fido out, take the pre-scented newspaper and a couple of sheets of fresh newspaper along with you. When you reach the outdoor potty area, place the pre-scented paper on the ground and the fresh papers on top of it. Use a rock to hold them all down if necessary. Then, give Fido a chance to do his business on top of the papers — and when he does, praise him lavishly.

Continue this routine until Fido's using the outdoor papers consistently. When he does, he's ready for the next step: moving the papers indoors.

Place a pre-scented newspaper beneath the top layer of fresh news-papers spread out on the floor in the potty area you've chosen. Make sure that the area you cover equals two or three side-by-side two-page newspaper spreads, and that the area is three or four layers deep.

At Fido's next scheduled potty break, take him to the papers instead of outside. Give him a few minutes to do his business. If he does, praise him lavishly; if he doesn't, wait 15 or 20 minutes and try again. Once he consistently uses the indoor paper, you can reduce the amount of floor space the papers take up.

Patience and encouragement is the key to making this transition work. You're asking your dog to make a big change after years of doing his bathroom business outside. Dogs don't like changes any more than most people do, but your enthusiasm and his eagerness to please you can help him overcome his reluctance.

From outdoors to litterbox

Moving a canine potty from an outdoor spot to an indoor litterbox is possible under certain circumstances, but it can be tricky. In fact, this switch can work only if 1) you live in a townhouse or single-family house, rather than in an apartment and 2) your dog's outdoor bath-room is located within your yard. For apartment dwellers and/or dogs with mobile outdoor potties, making this switch becomes way too complicated.

Start by bringing the new potty to the old potty. Just before one of your dog's scheduled bathroom breaks, put a little dog litter on his outdoor potty spot. Then, bring him to the outdoor spot and encourage him to do his business. Praise him when he does the deed(s).

Once he's consistently using the litter-covered outdoor potty, introduce him to the litterbox. Line the box with litter and place it next to the litter-covered outdoor potty area. Encourage him to investigate the litterbox and praise him lavishly when he does.

After your dog is used to seeing the litterbox in his outdoor potty area, introduce him to the idea of doing his business *inside* the box. Put some used litter or pre-scented paper in the box. When he does eliminate inside the box, let him know he's done the right thing: Lay the praise on thick.

Once he's using the litterbox consistently, stop placing the litter on the ground. This also is the time to start *slowly* moving the litterbox toward your house. Do so at a snail's pace, just a short distance each day. Eventually, you'll be able to locate the litterbox inside your home — and your days and nights of having to brave the elements to take your dog to the potty will be history!

If your dog balks at using the litterbox at any point in this process, take the hint: You're trying to make the change too quickly. Ease up. Make sure that he's mastered one step in the process before moving to the next one.

What to Do About Mistakes

Your puppy or dog undoubtedly is wonderful, but he isn't perfect. Inevitably, he'll deposit a puddle or pile away from the papers or litterbox.

When he makes this deposit, you will not be happy. In fact, depending on where your four-legged friend made his presentation, you may be very upset. But take a deep breath; take two if you need to. Repeat to yourself, "It's not his fault, it's not his fault." Take your pup back to his living area and don't say a word to him.

Then, go get a bunch of paper towels and the pet-stain remover you bought for just such an occasion. Clean up the evidence of the puppy's setback according to the directions on the cleaner. Make sure, too, that the spot is completely gone. Any leftover residue will lure your puppy back to the spot and prompt him to repeat his performance.

Whatever you do, don't scold, punish, or try to correct your puppy. And, of course, don't rub his nose in the puddle or pile. He won't have a clue as to why you're doing so. He will not connect your loud voice and angry gestures with the fact that he went to the bathroom a mere ten minutes ago. He won't understand why you're angry with him.

If he folds back his ears and puts his tail between his legs while you let him know how upset you are, don't think — not for a minute — that he's feeling guilty. Dogs do not know the meaning of guilt. Their consciences are perpetually clear. He's apprehensive, upset, maybe even fearful when you become angry, but he feels absolutely no remorse over doing what came naturally to him.

So, don't waste your breath; just clean up the mess. Then, consider what happened — but in doing so, don't focus on what your puppy did. Instead, figure out what you *didn't* do. Ask yourself what you could have done to prevent your puppy's accident can help get you started (see Table 8-3).

Table 8-3	Troubleshooting Fido's Accident
What Fido Did	*What You Should Do*
He peed when you weren't looking.	Don't let him out of his living area unless you can watch him every single second.
He pooped without warning.	Watch to see how he acts or what he does right before he unloads. That way, you'll be able to whisk him to his papers or litterbox before he has an accident.
He missed the papers.	Leave him a bigger area of newspapers for him to pee and poop on.
He missed the litterbox.	Change the litter and wash the litterbox regularly. Make sure, too, that the litterbox is big enough for your dog.
He peed on the same rug spot as yesterday.	Make sure you clean up the mess completely this time!!

When your dog has an accident, there's always a lesson to be learned. But you, not your pooch, are the one who needs to do the learning. That's because when your puppy has an accident, *you* are the one who's made a mistake.

One Method or the Other

It *would* be nice to be able to take your dog to an outdoor potty on sunny days, but have the option of spreading out some newspapers when the weather's lousy or you feel like sleeping late. Unfortunately, though, this convenience for you will only be a source of confusion for your dog — and a dog who's confused about bathroom protocol is anything but convenient.

A dog who hasn't figured out his household's bathroom rules expresses his confusion by having multiple accidents inside the house and not understanding what he's supposed to do when you take him outside. But you can avoid such confusion. Just decide whether you want your dog to do her business inside or outside — and train her accordingly.

That said, there *is* one situation when combining the indoor potty with outdoor training is necessary: if you're out all day and have a puppy who's less than four or five months old. A dog this young simply can't hold it that long, and it's unfair to ask him to try.

If your ultimate goal is an outdoor-trained dog, you and he will be better off if you can find some way to give your puppy a midday potty break: Maybe you can come home at lunch time, or hire a dog walker, or beg a neighbor to walk your canine baby at noontime. But if none of those options is possible, you have no choice: You have to let your puppy use the papers during the day. Spread out a few newspapers on the floor and count the days till he reaches that four- or five-month mark. When he does (or when you come home to dry papers every day for at least a week), you can stop putting down the daytime papers: He's ready to hold it all day.

A working person's guide to training a dog to go outside is contained in Chapter 10.

Another situation that may require your pup to use the papers temporarily is if he's under four months of age, hasn't gotten all his shots, and has nowhere to go outside but a public park or similar area that's visited by other dogs. Puppies are vulnerable to devastating diseases such as canine distemper and parvovirus, which can be transmitted through the bodily wastes and vomit that other dogs may leave behind. A series of shots protects the youngster from these potentially fatal maladies, but the shots don't take full effect until the series is completed. That occurs when the puppy is about 16 weeks of age.

So, if you're an urban dweller whose only outdoor potty spots are where other dogs do their business, heed your veterinarian's warnings. Don't take your canine cutie outside to pee or poop until she finishes her shots. Until then, let her potty on some newspapers. Once the shots are finished, you can either keep your puppy on papers if she's likely to be a small adult, or you can opt to move her bathroom outside. And if your choice is outward bound, check out Chapter 10.

Indoor training do's and don'ts

Here are some tips to make indoor training faster, more fun and more effective:

✔ *Do* consider indoor training if your dog is a very young city dweller, is a very small adult, spends a lot of time home alone, lives in a high-rise, or if you can't get around easily.

✔ *Do* consider your needs, your dog's needs, and the layout of your home when figuring out where to put the indoor potty.

✔ *Do* dog-proof your puppy's living area.

✔ *Do* get a crate for your indoor trainee, even if he doesn't have to "hold it" for as long as his outdoor-trained neighbor does.

✔ *Do* be patient if you decide to switch your dog from an outdoor potty to doing his business on the papers.

✔ *Don't* think that indoor training is just for puppies.

✔ *Don't* let your puppy roam around your home unless you're there to watch him every single minute he's doing so.

✔ *Don't* use slick color inserts for your puppy's potty; stick to newsprint.

✔ *Don't* leave stray newspapers on the floor if your dog is paper-trained.

✔ *Don't* get angry at your puppy for making a mistake; get mad at yourself for giving him a chance to do so.

✔ *Don't* try to teach your puppy to be an indoor-outdoor dog. Commit yourself (and him) to just one housetraining method.

✔ *Don't* try to teach your dog and cat to use the same litterbox.

✔ *Don't* take your litter trainee outside for a walk or for playtime until *after* he's done his business in the litterbox.

Chapter 9

Outdoor Training

- -

In This Chapter

▶ Opting for outdoor training

▶ Choosing an outdoor potty area

▶ Teaching with — and without — the crate

▶ Teaching puppies versus teaching adult dogs

▶ Dealing with mistakes

- -

1 didn't know this would happen — but by teaching my dog, Cory, to potty outside when he was a puppy, I'm staying in shape now.

I'm like any other suburban working mom: too much to do and not enough time in which to do it. For me, the name of the game is to stay on top of my all-too-full schedule, if not ahead of it. And the way to do that is to multitask: to do at least two things at the same time.

Cory helps me to do that. That's because at around 6 each morning, he and I head out for a walk, but not just any walk: We power-walk together for 20 to 30 minutes. Beforehand, though, Cory preps for this more-than-brisk trek through our subdivision by emptying his tanks almost immediately — the better to keep pace with me. And thanks to Cory's need to get that a.m. potty break, I make myself get up and out for the stay-in-shape exercise I need.

Of course, Cory's outdoor walks are far more than simply a time management tool for his human companion. There are plenty of other reasons to him and for other dogs to do their bathroom business outdoors.

How Outdoor Training Works

Outdoor training is the process of teaching your dog to eliminate *only* when he's outside. You can consider your pooch to be successfully outdoor-trained if he consistently holds his poop and pee until you take him outside — or he takes himself there.

Achieving such success can be surprisingly simple. You simply encourage Fido to do his business in the great outdoors, and do everything possible to prevent him from doing it indoors. Within a matter of weeks or even days, Fido will understand that it's okay to potty outside and will take it upon himself to make sure that he doesn't eliminate inside.

Outdoor training needn't be difficult, but it does require time and attention from you. Throughout the training process, you must keep an eagle eye on your four-legged friend to make sure that she doesn't poop or pee inside the house. When you can't do that, you need to put her some place, such as in a crate, where she's highly unlikely to eliminate.

When to Opt for Outdoor Training

There's one very good reason to consider keeping a dog's bathroom business outdoors: not wanting to deal with dog doo inside one's house.

Face it. No one truly likes to deal with canine waste (I'm having fun writing about it, but that's a whole other issue). Doggie doo stinks, and so does doggie pee. Plus, both stain any fabrics that they touch. Worst of all, they're each full of germs, bacteria, and other unlovely organisms that can literally sicken both your dog and yourself.

There are other good reasons to teach a dog to limit his bathroom maneuvers to outdoor turf. For one thing, the owner of an outdoor-trained dog doesn't have to allocate one bit of indoor floor space to newspapers or litterboxes. In addition, the outdoor potty can go just about anywhere that you and your dog go; all you need are some bags with which to perform cleanup. Finally, outdoor time with your dog is good for both your mental health and his.

To Crate or Not to Crate

I'm a big fan of using a crate to housetrain a puppy or a dog — especially a dog who's taking an outdoor path to achieving superior bathroom manners.

More than any other single piece of equipment, the crate will teach your puppy to keep her floodgates shut when she's inside your house. That's because the crate functions as a safe, secure den for her, and she'll do just about anything to avoid eliminating there. So by putting your puppy in the crate when you can't watch her, you're teaching her two crucial housetraining lessons: how to hold her poop and pee for a little while, and how to tell you when she can't hold it any longer.

But crating your puppy doesn't mean that you have to isolate her. In fact, the beauty of the crate is that you can confine your puppy, but you can move that confinement all over the house. When Cory was a puppy-in-housetraining, I'd keep his crate in my home office so that he could be with me while I worked. At meal times, I'd move the crate upstairs to the kitchen while my husband and I cooked, and into the dining room while we ate. After dinner, the crate and Cory would move downstairs into the family room, where we all watched TV. And at bedtime, the crate — with Cory in it, of course — would join my husband and me in our bedroom.

Speaking of bedrooms, please stifle any misgivings you may have over having your puppy share your boudoir. So what if you and your significant other engage in the act of love while your canine companion watches? Puppies and dogs are very discreet. Trust me: Your puppy won't tell anyone what you were doing. She may even sleep through the whole thing.

Not only will having your pooch in your bedroom not hurt your reputation, she'll benefit in countless ways. For one thing, having her nearby will make it much easier for you to hear her whine or cry if she needs to eliminate in the middle of the night. Moreover, sleeping in your room will give her an extended period of time with you, her new friend and leader. That time may not seem like a big deal to you. But for a puppy who's coping with the sudden loss of her mama and littermates, the knowledge that you're nearby makes that loss easier to bear.

If she can't use the crate

For some unfortunate dogs, the crate is not an effective potty-training tool. A puppy from a pet store, for example, may have come from a puppy mill where she had to eat, drink, and sleep amid her bodily waste. For such a puppy, the crate doesn't represent any kind of safe haven, much less a place to develop self-control. In fact, the opposite is the case: A puppy mill pooch may consider the crate the one place where she's *supposed* to do her business.

If your puppy appears to have no compunctions about soiling her crate — and if you're sure the crate's not too big for her — you'll need to be extra vigilant as you teach her basic bathroom maneuvers. Instead of confining her to a crate when you can't watch her, try putting her on a leash and putting that leash around your waist so that she can accompany you wherever you go. That way, you'll be able to watch her closely for signs that she needs to eliminate, and you'll be able to get her to her outdoor potty right away.

Don't just wait for those signs, though. Be proactive: Take her to the outdoor bathroom at least once every hour, or even more often if necessary. Make sure that you take her to the same place every time you go out and praise her whenever she does her business there. Use a pre-scented cloth or paper towel to help her get the idea. And follow the suggestions laid out in the "Outdoor Training for Puppies" and "A Matter of Timing" sections of this chapter.

Where to Put the Outdoor Potty

Until Fido figures out that the bathroom is outside — and can hold his poop and pee till he gets there — the backyard or some other outdoor area near your house is your best bathroom bet. That way, you and he won't have to go too far when he needs to poop or pee. Once your dog is consistently restricting his bathroom maneuvers to the great outdoors and lasts a couple of hours between potty breaks, you can expand his bathroom horizons beyond your property line.

The backyard is also the best place to start outdoor training a puppy who's younger than 16 weeks of age. That's because a young puppy hasn't received all the immunizations needed to protect him from potentially fatal diseases such as distemper and canine parvovirus, both of which can be transmitted through contact with infected dogs' bodily wastes or vomit. Until your canine youngster has completed his puppy shots, keep his potty in your backyard and don't take him for walks in any areas where other dogs may do their business.

Within the yard, a good potty spot is any place that's fairly close to your house and is easy to clean. Dogs don't like dirty bathrooms any more than people do, and your pooch won't want to use his designated toilet area if it's full of yesterday's output. Plan to clean up your dog's potty area once a day, at the very least.

Cleaning up takes on added importance once you start taking your dog to public places. If your dog poops in a public area, you *must* clean it up immediately thereafter. Most communities have enacted compulsory cleanup statutes, better known as pooper-scooper laws, for very good reasons: Dog poop is gross, and it carries disease-bearing organisms.

But even if your town or city doesn't have pooper-scooper laws on its books, common courtesy demands that you pick up your pooch's poop. Courtesy also demands that you not let your dog eliminate on someone else's lawn, and that you dispose of your dog's waste properly, no matter where he has deposited it.

For the scoop on cleanup equipment and techniques, check out Chapter 6.

Outdoor Training for Puppies

The great thing about outdoor training is that you can start doing it right away. And if you're really lucky, your puppy's breeder has started the process for you.

Many breeders start introducing puppies to outdoor potties when the pups reach the ages of four or five weeks. This age is the time when the mama dog is starting to push the puppies out of the den so that they don't do their business anywhere nearby. A good breeder often will give the mother some help by taking the puppies outside in nice weather and encouraging them to eliminate there.

But if your breeder hasn't started outdoor training, you can set the process in motion even before you and your puppy hit the road and head for home. Start by asking the breeder to give you a piece of paper towel or cloth that's scented with a bit of the puppy's urine. You'll use this pre-scented cloth to help your puppy learn where he can potty.

Then, as soon as the two of you arrive home from the breeder's, take your puppy to the outdoor potty area you've chosen. Car rides often trigger a puppy's I've-got-to-potty-right-now reflex — so let him do the doo and/or take a whiz before you head into the house. Place the pre-scented cloth on the ground and let your puppy sniff it. Then, when your puppy opens her floodgates and/or makes a solid deposit, praise her enthusiastically. Let her know that she's done exactly what you wanted her to do.

If she doesn't go, give her a little more time to explore. And even if she does eliminate, don't head back into the house right away. Many puppies need to pee two or three times during a potty break before they're completely empty.

If the outdoor potty area is in an unfenced area of your yard, leash your puppy before taking her to do the doo.

After she's done her business, take your puppy and let her explore your abode for a little while — but keep an eagle eye trained on your new friend. The reason: You need to watch for any signal that she's about to do a repeat potty performance. If she calls a sudden halt to her investigations, begins to sniff in a direct and purposeful manner, starts walking around in a circle, and/or actually begins to drop her bottom downward, she's just seconds away from unloading! Quickly — and I do mean quickly — scoop her up and take her outside to the same spot she anointed or pooped on earlier. The odor of her previous encounter probably will prompt her to do an encore there. When she does, praise her lavishly.

If for some reason you don't see any signs that she's about to go, and she surprises you with a little puddle or pile, say nothing. Simply clean up the mess — and promise yourself that you'll watch your little darling more carefully in the future.

After your puppy explores her new home for about an hour, she'll probably be pretty tired. Put her in her crate so that she can snooze for a little while. Do keep an eye on her, though, so that you can see when she wakes up. That's because a puppy who's just up from a nap is often a puppy who needs to pee. Take your little sleepyhead to her potty spot, and when she does her business, praise her.

For your puppy's first few days in your home, take her out every hour or two. Note when she goes and whether she poops, pees, or does both. At the very least, you'll probably find that she needs a bathroom break after every meal, naptime, and vigorous play session. In any case, you're likely to see a pattern emerge that will help you anticipate when your new family member needs to eliminate. You can use that knowledge to create a sleeping, feeding and bathroom schedule that will help your four-legged friend become a housetraining expert in a surprisingly short time.

What to Do When Your Puppy Potties

The way you behave while your puppy potties can either speed up or slow down his outdoor housetraining progress. That's because puppies have very short attention spans, and they can have a hard time staying focused during their potty breaks. Your behavior can either help your little guy get down to business — or make him forget to do his business.

To help your puppy concentrate on bathroom activities, get him thinking about those activities before you reach the potty spot. As the two of you head out to your pup's bathroom ask him, "Do you want to go potty?" in a happy, high-pitched voice, or announce to him, "It's potty time!" in a lively, can't-wait-to-get-out there tone of voice. Use the same expression and same tone of voice every time you take little Fido out, and soon he will associate both with heading out to the bathroom.

Do take the fastest, most direct route to the potty area — and use the same route every time your puppy needs a bathroom break. Here again, your consistency will condition little Fido to expect that when he walks that way, he's going to eliminate shortly thereafter.

When the two of you arrive at the potty spot, though, don't do anything. Don't talk to your puppy and don't play with him. Let him walk around a little bit, but don't let him leave the area until he's done his business.

As your little guy squats (male puppies don't start lifting their legs to pee until they're older, and most females never do), give him a command such as "Go potty" or "Do your business." Repeat this phrase every single time he eliminates. By doing so, you'll up your puppy's chances of learning to pee and poop on command — a handy skill for him to have.

More info about how to teach your dog to poop and pee on command — and what to do if he's one of those dogs who can't or won't acquire this skill — is in Chapter 11.

As soon as your puppy is finished, praise him for his performance. Take him for a walk, play with him, and indulge in a love fest. You've both earned it!

What should you do if you see your puppy start to potty inside? In two words: Distract her. Clap your hands, wail like a banshee, squeal "Oh nooooooooo!" — do anything to interrupt what she's about to do to your carpet or floor. Then, get her to the outdoor potty as fast as you can. Praise her if at that point she finishes what she started to do inside.

A Matter of Timing

Putting your puppy on a regular potty schedule will shorten his house-training learning curve considerably. Why? Because your pup, even at his young age, is a creature of habit. He learns through repetition. If you take him out to pee and poop at the same times each and every day, his body will become accustomed to that schedule. He'll be conditioned to do his business at the times you want him to do it.

A regular potty schedule also eases your job as your dog's caregiver. That's because a change in a dog's regular bathroom behavior often signals that he's sick. But if your dog doesn't exhibit such behavior — in other words, if he potties unpredictably — you won't be able to pick up any such signals.

When you put together a potty schedule for your puppy, keep in mind that most juvenile canines need to poop and/or pee at the following times:

- ✔ When they wake up
- ✔ After energetic playing
- ✔ After meals

Armed with this knowledge, along with your observations of your dog's own individual potty pattern, you can create a schedule that gives your puppy enough time to pee or poop, but also gives you some predictability. Table 9-1 shows how you might structure a schedule for a three-month-old pup:

Table 9-1 Outdoor Training Schedule for Three-Month-Old Puppy

Time	Tasks
7:00 a.m.	Get up.
	Take puppy outside.
	Put puppy in crate.
7:30 a.m.	Feed puppy.
	Offer water.
	Take puppy outside.
	Play with puppy up to 15 minutes.
	Put puppy in crate.
Midmorning	Offer water.
	Take puppy outside.
	Play with puppy up to 15 minutes.
	Put puppy in crate.
Noon	Feed puppy.
	Offer water.
	Take puppy outside.
	Play with puppy 15 to 30 minutes.
	Put puppy in crate.
Midafternoon	Offer water.
	Take puppy outside.
	Play with puppy up to 15 minutes.
	Put puppy in crate.
5:30 p.m.	Feed puppy.
	Offer water.
	Take puppy outside.
	Play with puppy up to 1 hour and/or let puppy hang out with family in the kitchen.
7:00 p.m.	Take puppy to outside.
	Play with puppy up to 15 minutes.
	Put puppy in crate.

Time	Tasks
Before bed	Take puppy outside.
	Put puppy in crate.
During the night	Take puppy outside if necessary.

You may be groaning inwardly at the prospect of having to take your four-legged friend outside for a middle-of-the-night potty break. Alas, that is one of the few disadvantages of raising a puppy instead of an adult dog. A canine youngster who's under three or four months of age just can't hold her poop or pee for the entire night, any more than a human infant can sleep through the night without filling her diaper. So when your puppy fidgets, whines, or cries in the middle of night, know that she's probably got a very good reason to do so. Heed her plea and take her out. And know that, as she gets older, your puppy won't need to go outside in the middle of the night. The same will be true of these midmorning, midafternoon, and 7 p.m. pit stops, as well as the noon-time feeding.

Part IV contains details on when and what to feed a dog.

This schedule requires someone to be home during the day to give the puppy daytime potty breaks. If you can't be your little darling's day-time bathroom escort, check out Chapter 10.

What if she doesn't go?

Sometimes, a puppy just won't eliminate — even though you think it's time for her to do some doo. If you've been out for more than five minutes and your puppy hasn't pooped or peed, take her back inside. But watch her like a hawk; do not take your eyes off her. Look for signs that she needs to go: circling, pacing, intense sniffing, a sudden stop in the middle of an activity. The second you see any such signs, get her back outside.

If you can't watch her, put her in her crate.

Whether she's in her crate or out on the floor with you, take her out again after 20 minutes. If she goes, praise her and take her back inside for some supervised play time. If she doesn't go, put her back in her crate, wait another 20 minutes or so, and head back outside. Eventually she *will* go; she can't hold that poop or pee for-ever. Praise her lavishly when she finally unloads!

Outdoor Training for Adult Dogs

Teaching an adult dog to do his bathroom business outside is similar to teaching a puppy. The difference between the two is that the adult dog doesn't need nearly as many bathroom breaks as a puppy does. But the principles are the same: showing your four-legged friend that his bathroom is outside and doing whatever it takes to keep him from eliminating inside.

Table 9-2 shows a sample schedule for outdoor training an adult dog.

Table 9-2	Outdoor Training Schedule for Adult Dog
Time	*Tasks*
7:00 a.m.	Get up.
	Take dog outside.
	Put dog in crate.
7:30 a.m.	Feed dog.
	Offer water.
	Take dog outside.
	Play with dog up to 15 minutes.
	Put dog in crate.
Noon	Take dog outside.
	Offer water.
	Play with dog 15 to 30 minutes.
	Put dog in crate.
5:30 p.m.	Take dog outside.
	Feed dog
	Offer water.
	Play with dog for 1 hour and/or let him hang out with family in the kitchen.
7:00 p.m.	Remove water.
Before bed	Take dog outside.
	Put dog in crate.

Once your dog has mastered his housetraining basics — which can happen in just a few days — you can eliminate the noontime potty break and consider giving him a little more freedom in your home.

How to Deal with Booboos

Yes, I know: Your puppy or dog is the most wonderful creature ever to have graced the planet (aside from yourself, your spouse, and your kids). But alas, even this paragon is not perfect; he makes mistakes — and many occur during the housetraining process. Despite your best efforts to teach him bathroom manners, your four-legged friend may not understand immediately what he's supposed to do (or not do). He'll demonstrate that lack of understanding by pooping or peeing inside your home instead of outside in his designated potty area.

Such mistakes try the soul of even the most patient dog owner. But no matter how irritated you feel, it's crucial to the ultimate success of your housetraining venture to not take your frustration out on your outdoor trainee. Take a deep breath and remind yourself that any mistakes he makes are *not* his fault. Then, take your little transgressor back to his crate, but don't say anything to him.

Once your four-legged friend is safely confined in his doggie den, grab some paper towels and some pet stain remover. Follow the directions on the cleaner bottle and clean up the evidence of your puppy's doodoo booboo. Make sure that you clean it up completely, because any leftover residue will entice your pooch back to the scene of his setback, and encourage him to do an encore.

Please, please, please, do not try to correct your erring pooch — by scolding him, punishing him, or rubbing his nose in his transgression. Any corrective efforts will be lost on him. He won't have the faintest idea as to what you're doing or why you're doing it. He will not connect your present behavior with the fact that he made a deposit on your living room rug only a few minutes earlier. He truly does not understand what is going on.

Folded-down ears, a tail between the legs, and a refusal to look at you do not — I repeat, do not — indicate that your dog feels bad about his bathroom booboo. The concept of guilt is not in your dog's emotional vocabulary. The body language you're seeing shows that he feels uneasy, distressed, maybe even scared. But guilty? Nah. So if your dog doesn't understand what he's done and doesn't feel any guilt, what should you do? Simple. Just clean up the mess. After that, think about what happened, and who should be blamed for your four-legged friend's mistake. Here's a hint: Instead of focusing on your puppy, focus on yourself. If he peed in your living room, ask yourself what he was doing in the living room unattended in the first place. If he pooped on your kitchen floor, ask yourself when his last bowel movement was, and whether you should have anticipated that by getting him outside earlier. In other words, try to figure out what *you* could have done to prevent your puppy's accident, and what you can do to make sure that he doesn't do an encore. Table 9-3 can help you get started.

Table 9-3	Troubleshooting Fido's Accident
What Fido Did	*What You Can Do*
He peed when your back was turned.	Never, ever let him out of his crate or living area unless you're prepared to watch him every minute.
He peed or pooped in his crate.	Make sure his crate isn't too big for him; it should be just large enough for him to stand up and turn around. Make sure, too, that he's not left in the crate for too long — three to four hours, max.
He pooped without warning.	Observe what he does immediately before he makes a deposit That way, you'll be able to scoop him up and take him outside before he has an accident.
He pees on the same indoor spot daily.	Make sure that you clean up completely!! And don't give him too much indoor freedom too soon.

Any canine potty accident contains a lesson to be learned — but the lesson is for you, not your dog. That's because when your puppy has a bathroom booboo, *you* are the one who's really goofed. By figuring out where you went wrong and making sure that you don't make the same mistake again, you'll make a giant leap toward having a truly house-trained dog.

Convenience Versus Confusion

After I've gotten my weekly TV fix of *ER* or *NYPD Blue* (and if you're reading this book after those shows have been cancelled, rest assured that I will have found new shows to replace them), the last thing I want to do is to take Cory out for his final whiz of the day. After all, it's 11 p.m. or later. I'm generally pretty tired by then. And if the weather's not to Cory's or my liking, my distaste for the late-night potty break increases. At those times, I fervently wish that I could just spread some newspapers in my kitchen or basement, march Cory over to them, tell him to do his bathroom business right there (and right away), and know that he'll comply.

But I never do it. I know better. I realize that Cory wouldn't have a clue as to why I'm spreading out those newspapers. He'd bypass them completely. Instead, he'd either have an accident in the house or (more likely) try to demonstrate that his bladder is made of iron. Either way, the result would not be good. If he had an accident in the house I'd be angry about having to clean it up, even though I'd have no one to blame but myself. If he tried to hold it, he'd boost his odds of getting a urinary tract infection — which would cause him some discomfort and force me to take him to the vet for an exam and some antibiotics.

That's why, no matter how tired I am and/or how awful the weather is outside, I take Cory out just before bedtime. We both sleep better afterward, even if it takes us a little longer to get to bed.

But what if I'd introduced him to both the outdoor potty and the paper potty when he was a puppy and just learning basic bathroom protocol? Couldn't I have taught him to be an indoor-outdoor dog then? Alas, I strongly suspect that the answer would be a resounding no, even for my canine genius.

Having an indoor-outdoor dog sounds wonderfully convenient in theory, but isn't worth trying to attain in practice. In your effort to achieve convenience, you probably just confuse your four-legged friend. A dog who's confused about his household's bathroom rules often expresses his confusion by having multiple accidents in the wrong places, and not knowing what he's supposed to do when he's taken to the right place. Such confusion is totally unnecessary, though. All you need to do is decide whether you want your dog to do her business inside or outside — and train her accordingly.

However, there *is* one situation in which you may need to provide a temporary indoor potty for your outdoor trainee: if you're out all day and have a puppy who's less than around five months of age. A dog this young simply can't hold it from nine to five, and it's wrong to even ask him to try.

If your ultimate goal is to teach your puppy to potty only outdoors, both you and he will be better off if you can a way to give your puppy a midday potty break. Consider coming home from work at lunchtime to take little Fido for a quick walk. Other alternatives include hiring a dog walker, begging a neighbor to walk your canine baby at noontime or (if your company approves) bringing little Fido to your office.

But if none of those options is feasible, you have no alternative: You *must* let your puppy use a potty indoors during the day. Confine your puppy to the kitchen with some baby gates or an x-pen and spread several layers of newspaper on the floor. When you're home, pick up the papers and take him outside to do any and all bathroom business. Meanwhile, count the days till he reaches that five-month mark. When he does (or the papers stay dry every day for at least a week), you can call a halt to the daytime papers: He's shown he can hold it all day.

Outdoor training do's and don'ts

Here are some ways to help outdoor trainee learn his bathroom manners faster and more effectively.

✔ *Do* set up your dog's crate before you bring him home.

✔ *Do* choose your dog's outdoor potty area before you bring him home.

✔ *Do* notice your dog's prepotty routine.

✔ *Do* take your puppy out at least every one to two hours when you first bring him home.

✔ *Do* use the same words and take the same route to the potty spot every time you take your dog out.

✔ *Do* praise your dog for using his outdoor potty spot.

✔ *Don't* punish your dog for having a potty accident.

✔ *Don't* give your untrained puppy or dog the run of the house unless you're right there to watch him.

✔ *Don't* place your dog in prolonged solitary confinement, either in the crate or in your yard.

✔ *Don't* distract your puppy when he's eliminating in his potty area.

✔ *Don't* expect your puppy to hold it all day while you're at work.

More housetraining guidance for the working person is contained in Chapter 10.

Another situation that requires temporary indoor training is if your little darling is less than four months old, hasn't gotten all her shots, and has no outdoor place to potty except for the communal latrine (such as a park) used by all the other dogs in the neighborhood. Young puppies can easily get life-threatening diseases such as parvovirus and distemper when they come into contact with the poop, pee, and/or vomit infected dogs leave behind. A series of shots protects puppies from these diseases, but the shots aren't fully effective until the series is completed. That happens when the puppy is about16 weeks old.

So, if you're a new-puppy owner who lives in the city, and whose only outdoor potty spots are where other dogs do their business, heed your veterinarian's warnings. Let your canine baby potty indoors until she finishes her shots. After that, you can move her bathroom outside. For the lowdown on moving an indoor potty outside, see the next chapter.

Chapter 10

The Finer Points of Housetraining

● ●

In This Chapter

▶ Knowing when your dog is fully housetrained

▶ Determining your dog's pottying style

▶ Teaching advanced bathroom behavior

▶ Coping with lifestyle changes

▶ Dealing with housetraining lapses

● ●

For every dog who's the subject of a housetraining horror story, there is another dog who quickly decodes the do's and don'ts of proper canine bathroom behavior. Fortunately for me, one of the latter dogs is my Sheltie, Cory.

Of course, I'd like to believe that one of the factors behind Cory's housetraining prowess was the possibility that *I* was doing something right. But whatever the reasons were, my outdoor-trained Sheltie guy had only a couple of indoor potty accidents during his entire housetraining process.

The funny thing was, it took me a long time to realize how well Cory was doing. I followed the outdoor training schedule outlined in the previous chapter until Cory was well beyond his three-month birthday. After that, I gradually cut back on the amount of time he spent in his crate and increased the amount of time he could run around the house. But I watched him like a hawk the whole time; he didn't get any unsupervised time at all.

Then, one morning when Cory was about six months old, he did something that surprised me. He and I were playing together, and although he wasn't due for a bathroom break, he suddenly stopped what he was doing. Then he walked over to the doorknob where his leash was hanging and tapped the leash with his nose before turning to stare at me.

I'm no rocket scientist, but I suspected that Cory was asking me to take him out. So I snapped on his leash and walked him outside to the median strip in front of our house. As soon as we reached the strip, Cory opened his floodgates. I was thrilled. And I figured that if Cory could tell me when he needed a bathroom break, I didn't have to worry about him having an accident in the house. In short, I was ready to consider him fully housetrained.

That red-letter day occurred six years ago. Since then, Cory has fully justified my faith in his bathroom abilities: He has not relieved himself in our house once since that long-ago day. No doubt about it: Cory's got the housetraining thing down pat.

When to Declare Victory

I'm not telling this story about Cory to impress you with either my training technique or his bathroom brilliance. (As you can see in the section, "Refusing to Pee on Command," which appears later in this chapter, sometimes he takes that brilliance a little too far.) The point here is that many dogs do show you that they understand what you expect from them with respect to potty manners. You just need to know what to look for.

Some dogs, like Cory, ask you to take them outdoors. But plenty of other signs indicate that a dog has mastered Housetraining 101. Here are a few:

✔ You haven't used your commercial pet-stain cleaner for weeks — whereas a month or so ago, you were using it almost every day. An unused bottle of cleaner probably means that your puppy pal isn't having any indoor accidents.

✔ You're consistently scooping up litter or cleaning up soiled papers soon after each meal that you serve your indoor-trained dog. This after-dinner (or breakfast) ritual means that your four-legged friend is eliminating on a regular schedule, and probably isn't having any out-of-the-litterbox or off-the-paper accidents.

✔ You come home from work and find that the newspapers that you left for your dog in the morning are unsullied by canine poop or pee. Moreover, the papers have stayed untouched not just just once or twice, but have consistently gone unused over the past couple of weeks. Consistently clean papers signal that your canine companion is holding his poop and pee all day and is confining his bathroom maneuvers to outdoor turf.

If your dog shows these or similar signs of housetraining mastery, congratulations to both of you on a job well done! By successfully teaching your dog basic bathroom manners, the two of you have laid the foundation for a rich and rewarding friendship.

The age factor

Even if your puppy shows signs of being a housetraining prodigy, think twice about declaring her fully housetrained if she's less than six months old.

A puppy under the age of six months may know when and where it's okay to potty. Physically, though, she may not always be able to keep from occasionally anointing your carpet or making a deposit on your floor — especially if she doesn't have fairly frequent access to her designated bathroom.

So even if your precocious little darling hasn't had an accident in weeks, don't assume that she can hold it at any and all times. And don't push the outer edge of her potty endurance envelope. Continue to keep her confined when you can't supervise her until she at least passes her half-year birthday.

And even then, give her only a little unsupervised freedom at a time. Just as you wouldn't let a newly licensed teenage driver attempt a cross-country trip immediately, you shouldn't let a newly housetrained puppy have immediate access to your entire house all day. Instead, confine your housetraining graduate to one or two rooms for a couple of hours or so and see how she does. Watch to see not only whether she holds her poop and pee, but also whether she decides to dig or chew on any forbidden household objects. If she passes muster, gradually give her more freedom. But just like with human children, don't give her too much freedom too soon.

But why stop there? Your dog can learn a lot more about proper potty deportment.

For example, maybe your dog can learn to ask to go out, if he isn't doing so already. And life certainly would be easier if your dog mastered the ultimate housetraining feat: doing his business as soon as you told him to. Think what it would be like to be able to take your dog out at night and not have to walk up and down your block until he decided to pee. Instead, you can march him to a particular potty spot, tell him something like, "Fido, do your business!" — and know that Fido would do just that.

If these and other canine toilet tricks sound intriguing, then this chapter is for you.

Your Pooch's Potty Style

Before you can boost your dog's housetraining skills to the advanced level, you need to decode his individual potty style. In other words, you need to know exactly what he does just before he actually eliminates.

Why is this knowledge so important? Because the key to teaching your dog advanced bathroom manners is being able to anticipate when he needs to take a whiz or make a deposit. Fortunately, most dogs provide clear signs that the urge to poop or pee is taking hold. The trick for you is to observe the signs that *your* dog exhibits. Then, you can put your observations to work as you teach him those fancy bathroom maneuvers.

- **The Statue:** Just before they do the doo, some dogs simply call a halt to any and all activity and stand as still as statues. Seconds later, they start to do their business. This no-frills approach to elimination is very common among young puppies, who frequently don't realize that they need to go until they're just about to do the deed.

- **The Pacer:** Many pooches engage in back-and-forth pacing before they eliminate. When such a dog is near his potty spot, he begins to walk in one direction, then turns around and walks an equal distance in the opposite direction. Depending on how badly he needs to go, he may walk back and forth once or twice — or as many as a dozen times.

    Many a Pacer starts his prepotty routine by walking as far as five or six feet in each direction. As the urge to go strengthens, he gradually shortens the pacing distance until he's only trotting a few inches back and forth. At that point, the dog eliminates. The speed at which a Pacer does his thing varies, although a speedy pace usually indicates that he'll be unloading momentarily.

- **The Circler:** Quite a few dogs start walking around in circles just before they eliminate. The size of these prepotty circles varies: Some have diameters that aren't much bigger than the dogs themselves, while other circles may sport diameters of several feet. Speed varies, too — although, just like with the Pacer, the faster the circling, the more imminent the potty event usually is. In fact, some Circlers will literally run rings around their people just before they potty.

- **The Sniffer:** Almost every dog engages in some sort of prepotty sniffing before he actually does the deed. Some dogs sniff before beginning to circle or pace, while others confine their prepotty maneuvers to intense snuffling of a particular spot just before they pee on it.

    As with circling and pacing, a dog's sniffing speed varies greatly, depending on how intense the urge to eliminate is. Generally, a dog who's simply moving his nose along the ground in a leisurely manner is still searching for what he considers to be a proper place to potty. However, intense, concentrated sniffing of a specific spot often indicates that a dog is about to anoint that spot.

> ✔ **The False Alarmist:** Some dogs are so particular about where they do their business that they engage repeatedly in one or more of the prepotty maneuvers outlined in the preceding list, only to stop before actually eliminating. Still, you can decode such a dog's prepotty behavior. A good general rule, in addition to those already described, is this: The more intensely and purposefully the dog is performing his prepotty maneuver, the more likely he is to actually poop or pee.

Some dogs adopt more than one potty style not only throughout their lives, but even within the same potty break. For example, Cory tends to be a Circler before he pees, but is more of a Pacer before he poops.

In any case, once you've identified your own canine companion's potty style(s), you're ready to teach him some advanced bathroom manners, starting with peeing on command.

Peeing on Command

Picture this: a dark and stormy night. You and your canine companion have spent a blissful couch-potato evening. Now it's almost bedtime, but instead of moving directly from sofa to bed you've got one final task to accomplish: taking your dog out for his last potty break of the day. And you're dreading it.

During most weather, you don't mind the end-of-the-day trip outside to your dog's potty spot. On nights like this one, though, the p.m. pit stop is quite another matter. Like most dogs, your special friend dislikes doing his business in the rain. Add some wind and cold, and the dislike mushrooms into out-and-out hatred. At such times, you just know that when you let him out to do his business, he'll stand next to the door, shiver, and attempt to look pitiful. Under no circumstances will he allow the damp ground to even brush against his hindquarters. And there's no way that he will actually unload in the rain.

Having you with him doesn't spur your pee- or poop-retentive pooch, either. What happens instead is that the two of you get to stand outside and get soaked together. That's not my idea of quality time, and probably not yours either.

These are the times when teaching your dog to pee on command comes in handy. The theory behind this maneuver is simple: You help your dog associate a command — a kind of "potty prompt" — with the act of urinating. When your dog makes that connection, he'll pee when you tell him to. Thus, when you and Fido are out in the rain, you simply march together to the potty spot, you tell Fido to pee, and voilà! He does.

In fact, your newly housetrained puppy may already do pee when you tell him to, if you followed the instructions for outdoor training in Chapter 9. But even if your four-legged friend hasn't mastered this maneuver, it's possible to teach even an adult dog with fully entrenched bathroom habits to do his business when told to. Here's how:

1. **Pick a potty prompt.**

   It's worth taking the time to consider this decision carefully. The ideal bathroom command is a phrase that you can use without embarrassment. For example, you may feel more comfortable telling your dog, "Fido, do your business," instead of "Fido, go take a leak."

   Be careful, too, that the prompt is a phrase that you'll use *only* when telling Fido to pee. A more general-sounding prompt, such as "Hurry up," can bring unwelcome results, such as Fido anointing the carpet at the same time you're telling your children to get out the door so that they won't be late for school.

2. **Take your dog to his potty spot the next time he has to do his bathroom business.**

3. **Watch for prepotty signals.**

   If you've taken the time to acquaint yourself with his potty style, you'll know what to look for (see preceding section). Then, when he starts those maneuvers, get ready to see him pee.

4. **Give the prompt as soon as your dog starts to pee.**

5. **Praise him lavishly when he's finished.**

Within a couple of weeks, he should make the connection between the potty prompt and the act of urinating and respond accordingly.

Refusing to Pee on Command

I have a confession to make. Although I am familiar with the mechanics of teaching a dog to urinate on command, my own canine companion just won't do it.

Some of my friends tease me about Cory's refusal to learn this maneuver. They want to know how I can possibly write a book about housetraining if I can't even get my own dog to piddle when prompted. But according to at least one expert, I shouldn't consider my inability to teach Cory a potty prompt to be a failure on my part, or a lack of intelligence on his part.

Dr. Paul McGreevy, a veterinary behaviorist at the University of Sydney, Australia, says that some dogs just may not be interested in learning to pee on cue. The reason: For such dogs, the act of urinating means a whole more than just emptying their bladders.

For example, Dr. McGreevy says, certain male dogs actually value their urine. When it comes to dispensing pee, says Dr. McGreevey, such a dog "sprinkles it like holy water onto only the very best substrates selected on the basis of size, prominence and pre-existing odors. Imposing bladder evacuation at times and places other than those of [this dog's] choice is clearly going to be more difficult than with [most female dogs]. Their motivations are different."

What Dr. McGreevy means is that for some dogs, urinating is much more than a matter of relieving themselves. For these canines, taking a whiz takes on additional meanings. To these pooches, their pee is their calling card — their announcement at a local street corner that they have been at that corner. Such dogs also sniff the ground, the pole beneath the corner stop sign, and just about any other vertical object to determine whether other dogs have left *their* calling cards behind.

A dog can tell a lot about another dog simply by sniffing a drop of that dog's pee. For example, one sniff of a local canine potty place can tell a romance-seeking male dog not only whether ladies have been in the area, but also whether those ladies are in the mood for love. (In other words, whether they're in heat.)

To make matters worse, some dogs' prepotty behavior is, to put it mildly, erratic. As an example, I've already noted that Cory tends to be a Circler before he pees and a Pacer before he poops. (See the section "Your Pooch's Potty Style," earlier in this chapter.) However, he sometimes offers no warning at all that he's going to eliminate. He'll just be walking along when suddenly he'll stop and do the deed before I've even realized what's going on. Other times, he'll pull so many false alarms that I give up trying to anticipate when he'll actually go.

And at the times that I'd most like for Cory to pee when I tell him to — like late at night and/or during a downpour — my Sheltie guy decides to vie for the title of Mr. Iron Bladder. Be it hail or snow, rain, or sleet — when the weather's bad, Cory tends to shut his floodgates tight. If I get uptight or angry over this pee-pee retentive behavior, he makes it clear that he thinks any sort of walk is a bad idea. He actually tries to pull me back into the house.

But even if your dog, like Cory, defies your efforts to teach him a potty prompt, you can still speed up his pee-pee process. Here's how:

- ✔ **Fake him out.** So what if it's raining? If you act as if walking in a downpour is more fun than playing fetch, your dog may believe you — and that belief may help him relax enough to go.

- ✔ **Stay loose.** A dog is more likely to do his business if he's relaxed rather than tense. For that reason, it's important that you stay relaxed, calm, and happy when you take your dog out for a potty break. If you feel yourself tensing up because your dog won't go, take him back inside and try again in a few minutes when you're both more relaxed.

✔ **Praise him before the fact.** If your dog shows the slightest hint that he's going to go — for me, it's when Cory moves from the sidewalk to the grass of the median strip — praise him lavishly. By doing so, you may help him realize that he's got the right idea and encourage him to follow through.

✔ **Find a familiar spot.** Often, you can jump-start your dog's urge to pee by taking him to the spot he anointed on his previous trip out. Chances are, he'll remember what he did there before — and do it again.

✔ **Find a communal potty.** If you can't remember why your dog went during your previous trip outside, take him some place where you know other dogs have pottied. The scent of previously deposited canine calling cards may prompt your dog to leave a "card" of his own.

Asking to Go Out

Some dogs, like Cory, teach themselves to ask their people to take them out (see Figure 10-1). But even these enterprising canines get a little help from their humans.

Figure 10-1: Your dog doesn't have to say a word to tell you when he needs to go out.

For Cory, that help came in the form of his leash, which my family and I hung on the same doorknob each and every time we came back inside from a trip to the potty. By always putting the leash in the same place, and by always using the leash when we needed to take Cory out, our Sheltie guy soon figured out that the fastest way to tell us what he needed was to go to his leash and tap it with his nose. You can do the same thing when you housetrain your dog.

Put the leash in the same place each and every time. Use the same words whenever you take your canine companion to his outdoor potty spot. Do exactly the same thing every single time you take your four-legged friend out, and you'll create the conditions that will help him figure out a way to tell you when he needs to go.

But if you don't want to play a waiting game, it's perfectly okay to take a more active approach to teaching your dog to ask for a potty break. Here's what to do.

1. **Get a signal maker.**

   Find something that can hang from a doorknob within reach of your dog's nose or paw and also makes a pleasant noise when the dog touches it lightly. A set of Christmas bells fits the bill.

2. **Teach the signal.**

   Every time you take your dog out for a potty break, ring the bells. Do this consistently, so that your canine companion associates the ringing of the bells with your taking him outside.

3. **Let him try.**

   Sooner or later, your dog will want to check out the bells himself. Encourage him to do so: Praise him enthusiastically if he even sniffs the bells.

4. **Heed his signal.**

   The first time your dog taps the bells with his paw or nose, respond promptly: Take him outside! Bring him to his potty spot and praise him lavishly if he goes. After a few times, your dog will connect his ringing of the bells with your taking him outside.

Don't let your four-legged friend fool you. If your puppy rings the bells but fails to do his duty once he's outside, march him back inside. Crying wolf is never a good idea — whether the crier is the boy from Aesop's fable, or your real-life canine companion.

Dealing with Lifestyle Issues

Housetraining isn't always a simple matter. Different factors can affect where and when you want your pooch to potty, as well as his ability to learn what you want him to know. In the following sections, I discuss how your lifestyle can complicate a housetraining enterprise and how you can help your four-legged friend cope successfully with those complications.

Outdoor training and the working owner

Housetraining is generally pretty easy when the canine trainee has a human around all day to supervise her progress. But that's not the situation in the vast majority of 21st-century households. Even most homes with children under the age of six are empty during the day, because parents work and their children go to day care or preschool.

This economic and social reality complicates any effort to train a puppy to potty outdoors. That's because a pup who's under six months of age can't be expected to hold his poop or pee all day long while his people are at work. Think about it: Do you spend an entire day — or even a half-day — at your workplace without making at least a couple of trips to the restroom?

At the same time, though, you can't give your outdoor trainee full access to your home. No way would you want to expose your carpet and furnishings to canine waste deposits.

But confinement in a crate isn't the answer, either. A couple of hours in a crate is reassuring to a dog, but that coziness can turn mighty claustrophobic to a dog who's forced to spend eight, nine, or even more hours there. Plus, the puppy who's crated all day is all too likely to poop or pee in the crate — which defeats the whole purpose of crating in the first place.

For that reason, the working puppy owner who opts for outdoor training needs to find some way to allow the puppy to eliminate during the day. You have several options from which to choose, including:

- **Hiring a pet sitter or dog walker.** Try asking an at-home neighbor you trust to walk your puppy and play with her once or twice a day or even to stay at the neighbor's home while you're at work. You can also contact a commercial pet-sitting service.

- **Going to doggie day care.** Many veterinarians and dog trainers offer some form of doggie day care to working owners and their puppies. In fact, some enterprising dog lovers are opening facililties devoted strictly to day care for pooches. Many retail pet Web sites include listings for such facilities; you can also obtain recommendations from trainers and vets.

> ✔ **Bringing your pup to work.** Some companies allow their employ-
> ees to bring their pets to work with them. Check and see whether
> your company's one of them — and if so, what the rules are. You
> may find that you can have a canine office-mate (and believe me,
> having a dog in your office makes work a lot more fun).

But if none of those options is available, you'll have to reconcile yourself not having your puppy trained to potty exclusively outdoors — at
least not right away. If you or someone else can't spell her during the
day, you'll need to combine paper training with outdoor training.

Here's how it works. You start by creating an indoor home-alone area
for your puppy — preferably someplace that doesn't have a carpet and
is easy to clean. The kitchen, laundry room, or bathroom would work
well here.

Then, cover the entire floor area with several layers of newspaper. Put
the puppy's crate and dishes at one end; leave the door to the crate
open. Enclose the entire area so that your pup can't venture beyond
the room. If your puppy poops or pees on the papers, clean them up
without comment. He hasn't done anything wrong by eliminating on
the papers, but you don't want him to think that you want him to use
the papers over the long term. And any time you're home, pick up the
papers and follow the outdoor training instructions in Chapter 9. If
you're headed out on a quick errand or otherwise can't watch your
little darling, put her in her crate.

Eventually, when your puppy nears six months of age or so, you'll be
able to bypass the papers forevermore. You'll know she's ready to
become a totally outdoor-trained dog when you repeatedly come home
from work at night and find nothing on the papers.

Moving the potty outside

Some puppies can't be allowed to potty outside, no matter how much
time their people can spend at home with them. These pooches live in
cities, where the only available places to do the doo are places where
other dogs have already pooped and peed. Exposing a puppy to such
places can be hazardous, because if those other dogs have certain
illnesses, germs and bacteria from those illnesses can longer in their
poop and pee, just waiting to pounce on your puppy.

To protect your little darling, you need to make sure that she has her
puppy shots — immunizations against diseases such as distemper,
hepatitis and parvovirus. Your veterinarian gives your puppy these
shots in a series, starting at about six weeks of age and finishing up at
about 16 weeks of age.

Until your urban puppy completes her shots, she can't be allowed to potty outdoors in places where other dogs might have pooped or peed. (If you have your own fenced backyard, it's fine to let her do her business outdoors.) After her last shot, though, you can move her potty from the newspapers to an outdoor spot.

Start by moving the papers themselves to an outdoor area and let your puppy eliminate on them. Gradually reduce the size of the paper until the puppy just goes to her potty spot and does her business *sans* paper.

Traveling with your dog

When motoring with Fido, remember to give him a bathroom break at least as often as you give yourself one: generally every couple of hours. Car travel is just as stimulating to the canine bladder as it can be to its human counterpart.

Bring your pooch's potty equipment with you: paper for the paper trainee, litter and litterbox for the litter trainee. For the outdoor trainee, bring a collar, leash, and bags for scooping.

For all canine travelers, it's a good idea to bring along the crate. Many hotels won't accommodate dogs unless they're crated. And no matter where you stay, the crate will give Fido an oasis of familiarity in an unfamiliar environment — and can help prevent accidents, too.

Changing your dog's diet

Throughout your dog's life, you may find yourself changing what he eats. A puppy eventually graduates to adult fare, a portly pooch may need to switch to a higher-fiber diet, and a finicky canine may need some new rations to perk up his appetite.

But no matter why you're changing your canine companion's rations, it's best to make such changes gradually — over, say, a period of several days to a week. The reason: Sudden changes can wreak havoc with your pooch's potty habits. For example, switching an overweight dog to a lower calorie, higher fiber diet can cause him to poop more often.

More about what your dog should eat and how he should eat it is in Part IV.

Coping with Housetraining Lapses

It happens to the best of dogs and their people: You come home from work and find that your perfectly potty-trained pooch has left a little pile of you-know-what on the living room carpet. Or maybe you find a puddle in your dog's bed after she gets up in the morning.

What's happened? What can you do about it?

There's lots of information on specific types of housetraining problems in Chapters 16 and 17. Generally, though, dealing successfully with a canine potty problem requires an owner to find out what caused the problem in the first place and then plot a course of action. Here's what to do if your dog seems to suddenly forget his housetraining lessons:

- ✔ **Clean up without comment.** If you come upon an unexpected puddle or pile, clean it up without saying a word to your dog. He won't remember what he's done, and he won't understand why you're displaying any anger toward him.

- ✔ **Clean up completely.** Use a commercial pet-stain cleaner to obliterate any canine waste. Any leftover residue — including just the odor — will tempt your dog to come back to the scene of his crime and commit a repeat offense.

- ✔ **See your veterinarian.** If your adult dog has more than one housetraining lapse after a long period of observing proper potty deportment, take him to your veterinarian. Very often, such lapses are the result of medical problems, not misbehavior.

- ✔ **Start remedial housetraining.** Once your vet rules out any medical causes for your dog's bathroom transgressions, start him back to square one with housetraining — and, in the meantime, keep him confined when you can't supervise him. And don't reinstate his house privileges until he's proven that he's reacquired proper potty manners.

Part IV
Making the Nutrition Connection

"WE'VE HAD SOME BEHAVIOR PROBLEMS SINCE GETTING 'SNOWBALL', BUT WITH PATIENCE, REPETITION, AND GENTLE DISCIPLINE, I'VE BEEN ABLE TO BREAK ROGER OF MOST OF THEM."

In this part . . .

*I*t's a simple housetraining fact: you can't control your dog's output unless you control his input. In other words, what goes in must eventually come out.

This part helps you housetrain your dog from within. You find out about what your dog needs to eat to keep his insides running smoothly, and you discover how his drinking habits can affect his bathroom manners, too. In addition, you see that how you feed your four-legged friend can be almost as important as what you feed him.

Chapter 11

What to Feed Your Dog

*Y*ou can't discuss the art of housetraining a dog — much less practice that art successfully — without also discussing what you are
going to feed that dog.

The reason is simple: What comes out of your dog in the form of pee or
poop is directly related to what you put in to him. Consequently, if you
control what you feed your four-legged friend, you can also exert some
control over his bathroom behavior. In this chapter, I elaborate on just
how that relationship works, and how you can take advantage of that
relationship when you teach your canine companion proper potty
deportment.

How Feeding Affects Housetraining

That what-goes-in-eventually-comes-out principle of housetraining
manifests itself in countless ways. Here are just a few examples:

✔ **What you feed** affects the size and consistency of your dog's
bowel movements, as well as how often he might need to do the
doo. For example, if your dog eats a lot of vegetables (and many
dogs enjoy veggies; as a for-instance, my own dog Cory adores
frozen broccoli florets), he'll probably need to poop more often
than the pooch who prefers more basic canine fare. The reason:
Vegetables contain relatively high amounts of fiber, and fiber acts
as a laxative — with predictable results.

Here's another example: Food that's high in salt is likely to make
your dog feel thirsty. That's not surprising when you consider how
parched a good baked ham meal can make *you* feel. Your dog reacts

similarly. Consequently, ingesting goodies that have a lot of salt in them, such as many table scraps, might send your pooch to his water dish more often than a dog who fails to score such delicacies. And the more times your dog tanks up, the more often he's going to need to empty his tank — in other words, to pee.

Even different types of dog food affect your dog's bathroom output. A dog who eats only dry food will have firmer, more compact, easier-to-clean-up stools than a pooch whose diet includes a lot of canned fare. Canned food contains a lot of water, which inevitably loosens up the stool.

✔ **When you feed** your dog directly affects when he'll need to go to the bathroom. A canine housetrainee who eats his dinner at 5 p.m. will need a potty break earlier in the evening than the dog who sups at 7 p.m. Experts explain that the very act of eating can activate a dog's *gastrocolic reflex*. In laymen's terms, that means the act of chowing down triggers your dog's urge to go.

✔ **How you feed** your dog can also affect his housetraining prowess. For example, a pooch who has to gulp his food amid a chaotic atmosphere may suffer from an upset stomach — which in turn can result in more frequent, looser, and tougher-to-clean-up bowel movements.

Details on how to feed your dog for maximum housetraining success appear in the next chapter. For now, I elaborate on what kind of food you can feed your dog, and how to decide among the many options available.

What Dogs Need to Eat

Like just about every other living organism, dogs need certain basic nutrients in order to survive, much less thrive. Those nutrients are protein, carbohydrates, fat, vitamins, and minerals. Here's why they need each, and where they can get them.

Proteins

Proteins enable the body to convert food into energy. Commercial dog foods contain several types of protein: meat protein (from animal organs or muscles); animal protein (any other part of the animal that contains protein, such as hooves and hair); and vegetable or grain protein (which comes from exactly where the name says it comes).

Not all proteins are created equal. A dog can digest meat or animal proteins more easily than vegetable proteins. And the more digestible the protein, the better it is.

The amount of protein a dog needs varies throughout its life. For example, puppies need more protein than adult dogs do, because they're still growing and need the extra energy that a higher protein diet provides. Protein requirements also vary between dogs. A Border Collie who spends her days herding livestock needs more protein in her diet than a Cocker Spaniel who spends most of his days napping.

Carbohydrates

Carbohydrates are also important sources of energy for dogs, people, and other living beings. They come from plants, which use light to create carbohydrates from carbon dioxide and water. This process, as you may recall from your junior high science classes, is called *photosynthesis*. Most carbohydrates come from grains such as corn, rice, and wheat. They may also come from legumes, particularly soybeans.

Fats

Fats are essential to maintaining healthy hair and skin. They also help keep a dog's body temperature stable and promote healthy digestion. Of course, too much fat in a diet — particularly when coupled with a lack of exercise — can lead to extra poundage on both pooches and people. Fats are contained in many foods and in supplements such as fatty acid capsules.

Vitamins and minerals

Vitamins and *minerals* enable the body to properly process those proteins, carbohydrates, and fats. They also help to sustain a dog's immune system, maintain coat quality, and prevent disorders ranging from bone problems to behavioral difficulties.

Vitamins and minerals may be incorporated into a commercial food or dispensed as a supplement in the form of pills or caplets. To be fully effective, vitamins and minerals must be balanced properly. For example, calcium supplements are not fully effective unless they are combined with magnesium.

Commercial Dog Foods

Years ago, dogs ate whatever people didn't feel like eating: table scraps, unwanted leftovers, and stuff otherwise destined for the garbage can. Canine companions of yore also weren't above rounding up their own protein sources. They'd kill other animals such as barnyard rodents or rabbits who made the mistake of straying into the fields where Fido liked to roam.

Getting what you pay for

The axiom "you get what you pay for" has probably never been truer than when it's applied to choosing food for your dog.

That bag of generic kibble you throw into your supermarket shopping cart may seem cheaper than the designer dog food available at a pet superstore or an online specialty retailer. The trouble is, you'll probably need to buy a whole lot more of the supermarket stuff before you approach the nutritional value of the premium fare. That's because the El Cheapo brand probably uses lower quality ingredients, like meat from diseased or decaying animals, or parts from other animals that people wouldn't dream of eating. That means the nutrients are of lower quality. For example, the cheap brand may contain less protein per unit than in a more expensive brand. Or the nutrients in the cut-rate brand are more difficult for your dog to digest.

The bottom line here is that premium brands sold at specialty stores generally deliver far more nutritional bang for your dog food buck. In the end, a relatively costly food may actually save you money: not only because your dog needs less of it but also because he's likely to be healthier, and thus need fewer trips to the vet. It's worth considering.

But just as life on the farm became a thing of the past for many people and their pooches, interest in breeding prize-winning dogs and other animals burgeoned. At the very same time that dogs could no longer scrounge up their own grub, their increasingly busy owners began demanding better fare than those table scraps and leftovers for their canine companions.

Enter the livestock feed industry, which began to expand its market beyond cattle, hog, and poultry producers to also include dog owners. The industry developed different combinations of grains and meat products into foods for dogs that were convenient to buy and easy to prepare. And as time went on and nutritional knowledge accumulated, the quality of some — but not all — manufactured foods improved.

Today's dog owner has a huge variety of commercial foods from which to choose for his dog, but they all generally fall into one of three categories:

  ✔ **Dry food.** This type of dog food consists of baked, bite-sized pellets derived from grains and meats. Commonly known as *kibble,* it lasts longer than any other type of dog food and is the easiest to fix: All you have to do is rip open the bag, pour some in your dog's dish, and set the dish down in front of him. If properly formulated, dry food may also be the best all-around commercial food for your dog, at least from a nutritional standpoint, and also provides the chewing action necessary to help keep his teeth clean. Finally, all-kibble diets are great for housetraining, because the poop from such diets is compact, dry, and easy to clean up. Unfortunately, though, dogs don't always want to go along with expert recommendations that they stay on a total-kibble diet. Some pooches find that all-kibble-all-the-time regimens are all too dull.

✔ **Canned food.** The moisture and aroma of canned foods will probably make them more pleasing to your pet's palate than plain old kibble will be. However, canned foods are more expensive than dry foods are, mainly because the can and the water inside (a *lot* of water is in canned food) make them more expensive to ship from the manufacturer to the grocery store. That extra water also means that it doesn't deliver as much nutrition as an equal amount of kibble does.

Another downside to canned food is that it doesn't last as long as its dry counterpart. Once you open the can, it needs to be kept in the fridge and used up within seven days. By contrast, dry food kept in an airtight container can last for weeks.

And finally, dogs whose diets include canned food produce poop that's bigger, wetter, and tougher to scoop than those who stick strictly to kibble.

Still, canned food can add some welcome flavor and aroma to kibble. It's worked well for my dog, Cory, who wouldn't be caught dead limiting himself to an all-dry-food diet.

✔ **Semi-moist food.** These foods look like people food — they may be shaped like hamburger patties, for example. They have less moisture than canned foods do, but more than kibble does. For some dog owners, semi-moist food may seem to provide the best of both worlds.

Your dog food choices depend mainly on your dog: his preferences, his age, and his lifestyle. For example, you might go for a higher protein food if your canine companion is a puppy and/or is very active. Lower protein foods are better for more sedentary canines. And if your dog doesn't like the brand you're currently feeding him, it makes sense to try another. No food, no matter how nutritious it is, will do your dog much good if he refuses to eat it.

But the fact that your dog likes her food isn't enough. It also needs to be good for her. Here are some questions to ask that will help you evaluate whether the food your pooch likes is good for her, too:

✔ **Is her poop firm and compact, or is it loose, bulky, and stinky?** If the latter is the case, your four-legged friend may be having trouble digesting the nutrients in the food. Consider switching to a higher quality food.

✔ **Is her skin dry and flaky?** That may mean there aren't enough fatty acids in the food. Consider switching to a food that has a higher fat content or consulting your vet about getting a fatty acid supplement.

✔ **Is your home-alone dog acting jittery? Does she seem spazzed?** The protein content in her food may be too high. Consider switching her to a lower protein product.

✔ **Is your dog passing a lot of gas? Is she constipated — or is she passing too much poop?** The food you're feeding may be too high in carbohydrates. Consider switching to a food that has a higher protein content and a lower level of carbs.

✔ **Is your pooch porking out?** Look for a higher protein, lower fat food. Pudgy pups (and adult dogs) are at greater risk for developing health problems than their slimmer canine brethren are.

You'll probably need to experiment some before finding a dog food that your canine companion likes. Just make sure, though, that all such experiments are very gradual. A dog who's switched suddenly from one food to another is very likely to be a dog with an upset stomach. To guard against seeing your dog's upchucked dinner grace your carpet, mix progressively larger amounts of the new food with the old over a period of several days.

Special Diets

Although the same types of ingredients appear in virtually every commercial dog food, the amounts of each vary. Many of these variances are deliberate. Pet food manufacturers combine these ingredients in different ways to create foods designed to address a wide range of conditions and life stages. These special diets include

✔ **Life cycle diets.** These dog foods are based on the premise that a dog's age affects what his nutritional requirements are. For example, a puppy needs more protein in his diet than an adult dog does because the puppy is growing. Life cycle diets often include food for young puppies, older puppies, adult dogs, and senior dogs. They've been a staple of the industry for many years.

✔ **Activity diets.** More recently, manufacturers have developed higher protein pet foods designed for certain high-energy canine activities. The canine candidates for these specialized foods include dogs that are extremely active or are involved in performance activities such as showing and agility, or female dogs who are either pregnant or are nursing puppies.

✔ **Condition diets.** Several pet food companies have developed a wide range of dog foods designed to aid in the treatment of a dizzying array of conditions. For example, one company has developed a food that's been proven to help extend the lives of dogs who have cancer, and other companies are finding that high-carbohydrate, lower protein diets may be a potent weapon in combating these dreaded diseases.

Meanwhile, several companies have developed product lines that aim to help pooches with food allergies. Such diets frequently eliminate corn, soybeans, or wheat from their foods, because some dogs are allergic to them. They may also substitute lamb or chicken for beef.

Other diets aim to aid in the treatment of conditions that range from accident recovery to weight management.

Home-Cooked Dog Foods

Sooner or later, no matter how committed you are to giving your dog commercial food, you're probably going to have to fix a doggie dinner yourself.

A common reason to give your dog a homemade meal is if your four-legged friend has a bout of diarrhea (and diarrhea is pretty common among dogs, so this possibility is more than likely). Among the remedies your veterinarian probably will suggest is to put your dog on a bland diet. This regimen consists of gentle, easy-to-digest foods guaranteed to soothe your pooch's tender tummy and put him well along on the road to recovery.

The foundation of this bland diet is boiled hamburger and rice. That's right: just plain, ordinary white rice, mixed with hamburger that's boiled till done and has the fat skimmed off.

The funny thing about hamburger and rice is that many dogs adore it. I won't go so far as to say that they love getting diarrhea just so that they can have the stuff. Nevertheless, you may find that the dog who appears to be nonchalant about getting his commercial dog food will glue himself to your side when you fix him that rice and burger dish. In fact, some dogs, such as my Cory, display clear reluctance to return to commercial foods after a few days of the hamburger-and-rice regimen.

At such times, I once again consider completely shifting Cory's diet from commercial fare to good old-fashioned homemade food. And every time — so far, anyway — I've ended up saying no.

The truth about table scraps

You see the warnings in just about every dog care book on the shelves. "Do not feed your dog table scraps!" they screech. Their reasons are virtuous and worthy: Rich, spicy food from the table will give your dog indigestion (and we all know what the results of *that* will be!). If you give your dog scraps from the table, you'll be encouraging him to adopt the obnoxious habit of begging. And no matter how you present those scraps, you'll upset the nutritional balance of his carefully formulated dog food.

Good reasons, all. There's just one problem: Almost everyone I know gives their canine companion food from their table at one time or another.

Holidays are one example. Most people can't bear to give our four-legged friends the usual kibble when they are feasting on Thanksgiving turkey. And even a pooch who's never eaten anything but dry food for dinner will turn those big-guilt-inducing eyes on her people when they sit down to an elaborate feast.

It's time to get real. Rather than stick with the no-table-scraps prohibition that everyone ignores, then, here are a few guidelines for giving your dog an occasional people-food feast:

✔ **Don't feed directly from the table.** The experts are right on this one; feeding anything from the table will encourage your dog to beg. I don't like being stared at while I eat, and you probably don't either. Don't let the habit start in the first place. Instead, put the goodies directly into your dog's dish.

✔ **Don't give him real garbage.** You wouldn't feed yourself the germ-ridden food thrown into the garbage, would you? Not fit for human consumption, right? Well, it's not fit for your dog's consumption either (even if he likes to try to raid the garbage can!).

✔ **Nix the fats and spices.** Foods laden with fats and spices — turkey stuffing, venison or other game fowl, pork, and veal — *will* upset your dog's stomach. Few events put more of a damper on a holiday dinner than having to clean up the results of that tummy upset, especially if that upset occurs near the dining table.

✔ **Bone up.** Uncooked beef bones make a nice treat for your pooch. Just be sure you spread out a big tarp or old shower curtain upon which your pooch can gnaw his bone, because they can get extremely messy. Never give your dog a cooked bone, though — it's too soft for safe chewing, and can cause your dog to choke.

So which table scraps are okay? If you're sharing Thanksgiving dinner with your dog, you can safely give him a little bit of the turkey *white* meat (the dark meat will be too fatty). For Thanksgiving and other feasts, rice, pasta, and vegetables also please many canine palates.

Why? Because putting together a nutritionally adequate, not to mention optimum, home-cooked diet takes more knowledge than I possess or have time to pursue. I'd feel obligated to consult a veterinary nutritionist and/or do an awful lot of reading to create a food plan that maintains Cory's glorious Sheltie coat, bright eyes, pink skin, and boundless energy. And frankly, I'm just too lazy to do it. (Understand that in my house, my husband does most of the cooking. I do not excel in the culinary arts and have no ambition to do so.)

Some of my dog-owning colleagues, however, are more dedicated, industrious, and facile in the kitchen than I. They do take the time to do the research necessary to prepare their pooches' meals at home. I admire them, even if I do not emulate them.

That's not to say, however, that Cory doesn't get homemade fare even though I haven't totally embraced the idea. I still boil up some hamburger — and for variety, some ground turkey — that I add to Cory's commercial fare. I sprinkle a little bit, no more than a tablespoon, into his dish. Sometimes I mix it in with the food; other times I just let it sit on top of the food. Either way, the aroma of that people food lures my Sheltie guy to his food dish like a magnet attracts steel. He eats everything with gusto — something he did not do when his dinner consisted of commercial food only.

If you decide to follow my lead and add a few homemade goodies to your dog's commercial fare, make sure that the home-cooked stuff accounts for only a minor portion of his total food intake. That way, you're less likely to upset the commercial diet's nutritional balance.

On the other hand, if you're more ambitious than I am and really want to try cooking your dog's food yourself, you may well find it's worth the effort. For example, if your dog has certain food allergies, being able to control the ingredients that go into your dog's meals may also help you control or even eliminate the allergic reaction. In addition, some dogs just don't do well on *any* commercial food. For them, home cooking transforms meal times and improves their health immeasurably.

 But if you're going to go all the way along the homemade route, make sure that you do your homework first. A good place to start is with your veterinarian, who's been trained in the art and science of canine nutrition. Talk with her, and together the two of you can map out a premium homemade diet for your dog. Check out the literature on the subject, too. One frequently recommended guide is *Holistic Guide to a Healthy Dog* by Wendy Volhard and Kerry Brown, DVM (Hungry Minds, Inc., 2000).

The BARF Diet

If you decide to find out more about canine feeding options, you'll probably come across the *BARF diet.* Rest assured, this food plan will not induce bulimia in your dog or anyone else.

To supplement or not to supplement

You may take a multivitamin every day, or calcium pills to prevent bone loss, or another medication to keep down your cholesterol count. If such supplements help you, wouldn't your dog benefit from the same?

Well, maybe. Then again, maybe not.

The resolution to the to-supplement-or-not-to-supplement dilemma really depends on your dog and how you choose to feed him. For example, if you fix your dog's food yourself, you may need to add certain supplements such as extra vitamins or fatty acids to ensure that he gets the proper balance of nutrients. On the other hand, devotees of commercial food may not need to add anything to the food at all.

However, even canine consumers of commercial food will need some supplements if they've been dealing with certain health conditions. For example, my dog Cory takes a high-level fatty acid caplet every day — as prescribed by his veterinarian — to help control a chronic nail condition he has. Vets may also prescribe fatty acid supplements for dogs whose coats and skin are excessively dry.

The bottom line on the supplements question is that the answer depends on your individual dog. Consider his needs carefully — preferably, with the help of your veterinarian.

BARF is an acronym for *Bones And Raw Food*. And it's just what it sounds like: a food plan in which you feed raw bones, raw meat, and fresh vegetables to your canine companion.

Proponents of this regimen believe that it's the closest to the food a dog would eat in the wild: the raw flesh and bones of killed prey, along with the plant residue in the stomachs of such prey. They believe that dogs on such diets live longer, healthier lives. Many people who have put their dogs on this diet report that their canine companions' teeth are cleaner, coats glossier, and overall health is significantly improved. I've seen some of these dogs myself — both before and after they became BARFers. Without question, the results are impressive.

On the other side of the issue, though, are many veterinarians. They worry that giving a dog raw bones — particularly poultry bones — can cause the animal to choke or develop internal injuries. They also are concerned about salmonella poisoning, which of course can befall people who consume certain raw foods. Starting and staying with this diet also requires a major time commitment on the part of the owner: to purchase the right foods (and to do so often — they need to be fresh) and to prepare them.

Anyone who wants to try the BARF diet for her dogs needs to do a lot of reading first. Good books to start with are *Give Your Dog a Bone* by Dr. Ian Billinghurst (self-published) and *Dr. Pitcairn's Complete Guide to Natural Health for Dogs and Cats* by Richard H. Pitcairn (Rodale Press). The latter book is available at Amazon.com and most book superstores. Billinghurst's book is available from www.dogwise.com from the author's own site (www.drianbillinghurst.com).

Your Dog's Drinking Habits

Like all living creatures, dogs need water just to live, much less generate any dog pee. In fact, a dog can go without food for weeks at a time — but the dog who goes without water for more than a few days will die.

Dogs need water for the same reasons that people do. Water is crucial to regulating the body temperatures of both the human and canine species. Just as important is the fact that water is the foundation of the body's internal transportation system. As the main ingredient in blood, water shuttles nutrients from the digestive system to anywhere else the body needs them. And as the main ingredient in urine, water transports waste products outside the human or canine body.

But while all dogs need water for the same reasons, the amount of water they need varies from pooch to pooch. Dogs who are very active and/or eat a lot of food — especially dry food — need to drink more water than more sedentary canines, those who eat less, and/or those whose diets include some canned or moist fare.

Healthy, housetrained dogs can regulate their water intake all by themselves. They'll drink when they're thirsty and not drink when they're not. Meeting the water needs of these dogs is simple: Keep water available at all times.

Keeping water available, however, does *not* mean just topping the water off throughout the day or week. A dog needs totally fresh water in a dish that's washed at least once a day. And you should change the water itself at least once a day, or any time you see stuff — for example, little bits of food residue — floating in the water.

Failure to change the water can turn it into a scummy mess that no pooch should have to drink. Failure to wash the dish can make it a breeding ground for algae, mold, and other unlovely critters that can throw your dog's body workings out of whack. Wash the dish daily with mild detergent and make sure that you rinse the dish thoroughly (so that your dog doesn't end up drinking soap). A daily dousing in the dishwasher is great.

Is all water created equal?

Maybe you've gotten into the habit of carrying bottled water with you wherever you go. If so, you're taking a significant step in maintaining or even improving your health. Having water with you on the fly helps you to fulfill the human body's need for as much as 48 ounces of water per day. Moreover, the bottled stuff is free of the harmful contaminants that can lead to numerous health problems.

Just as purified water can improve a human being's health, so can it do good things for the health of a dog. For example, veterinary urologist Marc Berkovitch, DVM, believes that switching from tap water to distilled water can help prevent the formation of bladder stones in dogs as well as in people. The reason: Distilled water doesn't contain any minerals, which are what causes the stones to form.

For that reason, Berkovitch recommends that any dog who's prone to getting bladder stones be given distilled water rather than the stuff that comes from the tap. And at less than a dollar a per gallon-sized jug, it's a lot cheaper than Evian — not to mention surgery to remove any urinary stones.

For the canine-in-housetraining, 24/7 access to water could pose a problem. That's because in order to anticipate when your dog might need to let some water out — in other words, to pee — you need to have some idea of when he took that water in. The best way to acquire that knowledge is to control his access to the water bowl. Make no mistake: The dog who's just learning basic bathroom manners needs frequent opportunities to drink. But you need to know when he takes advantage of those opportunities — and the best way to gain that knowledge is to give him a dish of clean water several times a day, at the same times each and every day.

Chapters 9 and 10 contain sample schedules for feeding and watering your housetrainee, and when to give him a bathroom break.

If your dog suddenly starts drinking more water than usual — and consequently starts peeing more often than usual — he may well be sick. Chapter 15 outlines some of the maladies that increased water intake may signify and what you can do about them.

To Treat or Not to Treat

Dogs love to snack and eat treats just as much as people do — but the question of whether to give a pooch in housetraining any treats may be difficult to answer.

Certainly a good case can be made for using treats to train your dog. They're a great learning incentive; I use them liberally when training my own dog and working with other people's pooches. You can use a treat to actually lure a dog into sitting or lying down on command. A treat makes a great reward for the dog who's learning to come on command and can jump-start your dog's learning process in countless other ways.

In fact, a whole segment of expert dog trainers uses treats as the foundation of their training philosophy, known in most circles as *positive reinforcement*. Proponents of positive reinforcement rely on treats and other rewards (such as a toy and/or lavish praise) to help a dog understand what a person wants the animal to do (see Figure 11-1). For example, suppose that you wanted to teach your dog to go to his bed when you told him to. A trainer from the positive reinforcement school might suggest that you leash the dog, give the command "Bed," and gently walk the dog to the bed. As soon as the dog is in the bed, you'd praise the dog and give him a treat. Eventually the dog learns the command and goes to the bed by himself. At that point, you start tapering off the treats.

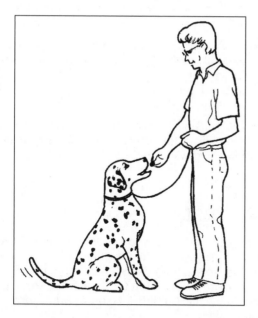

Figure 11-1: Treats can be a great teaching tool.

Many trainers and other experts — myself included — swear by treats as an unbeatable training tool. Treats are a gentle, not to mention tasty, way to jump-start a dog's desire to learn.

That said, however, I'm not sure that treats should play a prominent role in housetraining.

The reasons for my apparent self-contradiction? I've got two: First, giving lots of treats to a dog who's just learning his bathroom manners can wreak havoc with a dog's digestion and may prompt him to potty more often than would otherwise be the case. Second, when it comes to housetraining, a dog already has lots of incentive to learn what's expected of him. That incentive, of course, is his instinctive desire to not soil his den or his dining area. For those reasons, I don't recommend using treats to housetrain a dog.

However, plenty of people teach their dogs other commands at the same time they're teaching their pooches proper potty deportment — and dogs will learn those other lessons more quickly if they've got a tasty incentive dangling in front of their noses. Those reasons prompt the following guidelines for giving treats to the housetrainee:

✔ **Teach just before mealtimes.** Give your dog his lessons in sitting, lying down, and other maneuvers just before he eats. A hungry dog will have more incentive to learn than a dog whose tummy is full. And by giving him those treats just before mealtime, you probably won't have to get him to his potty immediately after his lesson. You can just feed him and bring him to his bathroom after the meal.

✔ **Adjust the main course.** Many treats — especially the commercial variety — are incredibly fattening. If you're giving your house-trainee commercial goodies during his other lessons, you need to reduce the portions you put in his dish at meal times. Otherwise, your pooch will pork out quickly.

✔ **Easy does it.** If you're using treats for training, soft-pedal giving your dog extra goodies at other times — no matter how much he might beg for them. That way, you won't put his gastrocolic reflex on overdrive.

Commercial treats

Those of you who decide to add treats to your dog's diet will find an incredible assortment of goodies to choose from. Regular supermarket aisles, pet boutique floor space, print catalog pages, and online pet store bandwidth are clogged with culinary offerings designed to please the most discriminating canine palate. Here are some of the more common types of commercial treats.

✔ **Biscuits and cookies.** From the been-around-forever offerings of Purina's Milk Bones to the elevated gourmet fare of Three Dog Bakery, biscuits and cookies jump-start the appetites of countless canines. The fact that most dogs love scarfing down biscuits and cookies gives these products a big advantage; another is that their small sizes make them easy for dogs to chew and digest. In addition, their crunchy textures provide good chewing exercise for dogs and can even help clean a canine's canines (as well as his other teeth).

The downside? Many biscuits and cookies are loaded with calories. Just as fast-food chicken can add inches to your waistline, so can too many cookies add unwanted poundage to your pooch. In addition, some treats can upset the nutritional balance that commercial dog foods offers.

If you're worried about upsetting the nutritional balance offered by your dog's commercial food, try a treat that carries the same product name as the main food product. Science Diet, which is manufactured by Hills, and California Natural, which is manufactured by Innova, are just two product lines that include treats designed to dovetail with their regular dog foods.

Another option for maintaining your dog's nutritional balance is to give him kibble for his treats. If your dog enjoys his dry food, individual pieces could make a nutritious, fuss-free treat.

Do not ever, *ever* give your dog anything that contains chocolate. Although most dogs like it (at least the smell!), chocolate contains an ingredient that's toxic to them. Even a small amount can put your dog in dire distress and could even kill him.

✔ **Chew treats.** Most dogs adore chomping on chew treats made of rawhide, pigs' ears, horses hooves, and other animal parts. In fact, some may adore them a little too much. These chewing maniacs may gnaw off and swallow big chunks of such treats, and those chunks can cause internal injuries. And even small pieces of these treats can cause digestive upsets. Bottom line: Balance your dog's delight in these treats with his tolerance for their downside. And if your dog has a sensitive stomach, don't offer them at all.

Homemade treats

If you enjoy making treats for yourself and the other people in your household, you may also enjoy making treats for your canine family member. Homemade treats offer several advantages over commercial fare, the biggest being that you have much more control than is the case if you rely on a manufacturer. When you make treats yourself, you know which ingredients (and how much of each) go into the treat — an important consideration if, for example, your canine companion suffers from food allergies. You can also control the size of the treat so that it's just right for your particular dog.

Like the idea of giving your dog homemade goodies, but don't know where to begin? Mosey on over to the World Wide Web's Google search engine. Type "dog treat recipes" into the keyword box. Then watch Google instantaneously dig out more than 300 sites that have multiple recipes to try on your four-legged friend. One caution, though: Most of these sites don't include any nutritional analyses — so feed sparingly, no matter how much your dog loves the results of your efforts. And if you're not virtually inclined, your public library undoubtedly has plenty of books on dog treats for you to peruse.

Want to make a fast, can't-miss treat for your dog? Get some hot dogs, slice them up thin, and bake them in your microwave until they're as crisp as bacon. Afterward, drain the slices on some paper towels. Feed these to even the pickiest pooch, and he will worship the ground you walk on — plus learn his doggie lessons faster than you dreamed possible. Do feed these nuked goodies sparingly, though — although hot dogs are delicious, they're not necessarily the most nutritious foods either humans or canines could eat.

Low-calorie treat options

Yes, you can give your dog treats without necessarily causing him to put on excess poundage. Here are some possibilities:

- **Vegetables.** Many dogs adore raw or frozen vegetables, and because they're so low in calories, they make a terrific treat for the plumper pooch. Good veggies to try are carrots, Brussels sprouts, broccoli, and green beans. Make sure that you offer small pieces, though, so that your four-legged friend can digest those greens and yellows easily. And be aware that vegetables contain fiber, which acts as a laxative. If you give your pooch too many veggies, he'll need to poop a lot more often.

- **Rice cakes.** They may seem utterly devoid of taste to you, me, and other human gourmands — but believe me, I have seen otherwise discriminating dogs go nuts over the prospect of getting a piece of rice cake. One Dachshund of my acquaintance starts barking madly for hers as soon as she sees one of her people getting the package out from the kitchen cabinet.

- **Low-cal commercial treats.** Some pet food manufacturers offer low-calorie versions of their usual dog treats. Try giving some to your dog if he doesn't go for the veggies or rice cakes.

Chapter 12

How to Feed Your Dog

*W*hen it comes to housetraining, knowing *how* to feed your dog matters just as much as knowing *what* to feed him.

Why? Because when you housetrain your canine companion, you need to regulate not only where your dog's bathroom output emerges, but also how it emerges. In order to control the "how" in that output, you need to regulate how the input — in other words, the food — enters your dog beforehand.

When to Feed Your Dog

Timing is everything in most enterprises, including housetraining. You want your dog to do learn to do his bathroom business at regular, predictable intervals. That's why it's a good idea to put your canine housetrainee on a regular potty schedule, at least until Fido masters his bathroom basics. To be fully effective, that potty schedule also needs to cover feeding times, because most pooches want to potty soon after they eat. Consequently, by making Fido's meal times predictable, you'll go a long way toward making his potty times equally predictable.

Why not free feed?

"How can I schedule my dog's meals?" you may ask. "I don't even schedule my *own* meals. Plus, my parents never bothered to schedule our dog's meals when I was a kid. We just put a dish of dog food on the floor every morning, and he ate whenever he wanted."

It's true that a generation ago, many people simply scooped a couple of piles of kibble into their dogs' dishes and left those dishes out all day for Fido to feast on whenever his stomach growled. Some people still do that, in a practice experts call *free feeding*.

Without a doubt, free feeding is a far more convenient way to give your dog his grub than remembering to feed Fido at certain times every single day. However, free feeding carries three major disadvantages, at least two of which directly affect a dog's bathroom behavior:

✔ **Lack of predictability.** If food is always available to your dog, you may have a tough time determining when he actually chows down. Without such knowledge, you can't really anticipate when he's likely to poop or pee. Consequently, the dog who eats whenever he wants may have more trouble learning his bathroom basics than the dog whose mealtimes are scheduled.

✔ **Lack of regularity.** It's tough to tell how much food a dog has eaten at any one time if he's got 24/7 access to that food. That means you won't realize as quickly whether your dog is eating his usual fill. That lack of knowledge may keep you from spotting potential health problems.

✔ **Too much autonomy.** By letting your pooch have unfettered access to food, you're foregoing important opportunities to reinforce your status as the leader of the pack. Every time your dog sees you prepare and serve him his food, he realizes that you are The Giver of All Good Things. That realization strengthens the bond you share and encourages his desire to please you, both of which help you to teach him the lessons he needs to learn — including housetraining.

A schedule for every dog

Although free feeding's not the best way to feed your four-legged friend, frequent meals will help keep him in the best of health — especially if he's a young puppy. A juvenile canine needs to eat more often than an adult dog does. But even an adult dog needs to dine more often than you may suspect.

✔ **Puppies under four months** of age should get at least three meals a day: morning, midday, and early evening. Water should be made available at meal times, plus a fourth time a little while after dinner. Take up the water no later than two hours before bedtime, though, or your pup will need a middle-of-the-night potty break.

✔ **Puppies from four months to one year** of age can cut back to two meals per day: one in the morning and one in the evening. And if they've mastered Housetraining 101, they can get start getting unlimited water.

✔ **Adult dogs** also do best with two meals a day plus unlimited water. Although many grown-up pooches do get by with just one big dinner each day, a twice-daily meal plan can help forestall a boatload of problems. For example, dogs, like people, tend to get sleepy after they eat — which means that the dog who gets both a good breakfast in the morning is more likely to nap than to trash the house if his human companion is gone all day. And a good dinner will help him sleep more comfortably through the night. (Could you sleep if your stomach were growling?)

The morning-and-evening regimen can also help prevent several physical problems. Some, such as flatulence, usually aren't serious. But one extremely serious condition, *bloat,* also can result if a dog scarfs a very large meal. Large dogs are more likely to be stricken with bloat (also known as *gastric tortion*) than smaller breeds are.

If, after a meal, your dog's stomach seems to expand, and he become restless, unable to lie down, and either pants or cries, get him to a vet or emergency clinic immediately. Bloat is a life-or-death situation — without prompt veterinary attention, a dog with this condition does not survive.

Before or after the humans eat?

Some experts suggest feeding your dog after the people in the house have their meals. They believe that making a dog wait for her meals underscores the fact that people outrank the pooches in the family pack. They also point out that in the wild, the alpha wolf generally eats before the rest of the pack does. Consequently, feed-the-dog-last advocates believe that alpha people should follow suit when feeding *their* canine pack members.

Other people find that feeding Fido before they eat works better. They find that a dog with a full tummy is less likely to try scoring table scraps from the human family members while *they* eat.

Still others favor simultaneous dining: letting the dog eat at the same time that his people do. One undeniable advantage to this option is that the dog is too busy eating her own food to worry about eating yours. However, the logistics of preparing human and canine cuisine at the same time could prove to be a challenge to people like me, whose multitasking ability is somewhat limited!

With the exception of that caveat, I don't advocate any one of these three dining options. This is one instance where the right answer varies with each dog and each family. I generally feed my dog, Cory, before the rest of my family eats — not because he begs for table goodies (we don't permit such behavior in our house) but because Cory has trouble concentrating on eating, and because the humans in our house tend to dine late. For those reasons, I give my Sheltie Guy his grub around 6:30 or so in the morning and 5:30 in the evening. During those times, the house is relatively quiet, which makes it easier for my distractible dog to focus on his food.

Where to Feed Your Dog

Choosing where to feed your dog depends mostly on what works for you. The most convenient canine dining room is one that's located close to the place where meals are prepared, if not actually in the same place.

For most households, that place is the kitchen. Placing the doggie dining room here offers several advantages to both you and your dog. For you, the big plus is that the kitchen is usually the room that's easiest to clean: a big consideration if, like many dogs, your four-legged friend doesn't eat all that neatly. For your dog, the big plus to kitchen dining is that the kitchen is where the rest of the household usually congregates. That means a lot to a social animal like your canine companion, who's happiest when he's hanging out with the other members of his pack.

If you're training your dog to potty indoors, don't feed him in the same place he does his business. Dogs don't like eating anywhere near their bathrooms. However, that prohibition doesn't mean you can't feed Fido in the kitchen just because his papers or litterbox are located in the same room. You should, however, place his dishes at least a few feet away from the indoor potty, so that he doesn't have to dine in the same place he does his business.

You can also feed your dog in his crate — and in fact, doing so can help your dog learn his basic bathroom manners more quickly. That's because crate-based dining gives your four-legged friend another reason to like this makeshift doggie den. In addition, eating in the crate helps a pooch learn to refrain from pooping or peeing as soon he's finished a meal. The reason, of course, is that he doesn't want to soil his den.

Many plastic crates include small dishes that can be attached to the inside doors. That's because airline regulations require that the dog be able to eat and drink while in flight, and plastic crates are designed to conform with those regulations.

Canine Dining Ambience

What sort of dining atmosphere do you prefer? Do you like a noisy, hectic, Grand-Central-Station eating experience? Or do you prefer a quieter, more low-key dining environment? Do you like eating with a crowd? With one or two other people? Alone?

Of course, there's no correct answer to any of those questions. Every response simply reflects the responder's personal preference. And that's exactly the point. You may have definite ideas about the ideal dining experience — and your dog might, too.

For example, Cory has made it clear to my family and me that he doesn't like to eat by himself. He's a semi-social diner; he likes knowing that I'm nearby while he eats his breakfast or dinner in the family kitchen. If I leave any of the rooms that adjoin the kitchen, he'll stop eating and come look for me. To ease his apparent worries, I've learned to stick around while Cory eats.

Moreover, my four-legged gourmand seems to prefer that dining experiences not be overly stimulating. Any household activity that diverts or excites him, such as someone taking the trash outside (he apparently believes it's his job to escort the trash-taker to the front door), will prompt him to stop eating — at least until the excitement has abated.

My husband, daughter, and I have learned to cater to Cory's dining whims. That seems only fair. After all, we've made it clear that we expect him to respect *our* dining preferences. For example, we've taught him that it's not nice to stare at human diners, no matter how much he'd like one of those diners to drop him a morsel or two. We also expect him to keep his distance while we eat; in other words, lurking around the table is strictly forbidden when humans are already there. Consequently, we feel justice demands that we be as sensitive to his dining preferences as we expect him to be to ours.

I truly believe that decoding a dog's dining desires can make for better bathroom behavior. A dog who's happy with his dining environment will eat more regularly — and a dog who eats more regularly will probably eliminate more regularly than a dog who's too distracted to attend to what's in her dish. Any way you look at it, what goes in eventually comes out — but what *doesn't* go in ultimately goes nowhere except to the garbage disposal.

But while dogs may have individual ideas about how they like to dine, there are a few canine dining concepts that apply to all pooches. Here are some ideas on how to make mealtime a good time for just about any dog:

- **Minimize stress.** Don't be afraid to cater to your dog's dining preferences, at least a little bit. Dogs who are stressed out while eating are more likely to have upset stomachs than those whose mealtimes are relatively tranquil. A pooch with a troubled tummy may get gassy or even vomit after his meal.

- **Separate siblings.** If yours is a multidog household, it's a good idea to feed each canine pack member separately — in different locations and/or at different times. That way, neither dog will feel the need to scarf down his food in order to keep the other pooch from grabbing his grub.

✔ **Let him linger — a little.** Your dog deserves a chance to savor his breakfast, lunch, or dinner. Give him at least 15 minutes to finish his meal. However, giving your dog an unlimited amount of time to eat is not a good idea. Doing so can wreak havoc with potty routines and thus defeat the purpose of setting up a feeding schedule. If your dog hasn't finished his meal in 30 minutes, toss it.

✔ **Wash those dishes.** No one, including your dog, likes to eat fresh food off dirty dishes. Be sure to wash your dog's food dishes after every meal, either by hand or in the dishwasher. Water dishes need daily washing, too.

✔ **Know when to get help.** If your dog's been gassy after meals but also is losing weight or has diarrhea, he may be sick. Take him to your vet to rule out any potentially serious conditions, such as inflammatory bowel syndrome.

All About Dishes

No discussion of how to feed a dog is complete without a little dishing about dishes. They come in a wide range of sizes and shapes. Your best bet is to choose the one that best fits your dog's size, age, and appetite. For example, a short-faced breed, like a Pug, does well with a wide, shallow bowl. A long-eared dog, such as a Cocker Spaniel, fares better with a narrow, deep bowl. Puppies of any breed may find the eating to be easier with a "flying saucer"-shaped bowl that has a raised center; such a bowl keeps food where they can reach it. An older dog or arthritic animal may eat more easily if his dish is raised up from the floor.

Next, consider the material. Experts give a unanimous thumbs-up to stainless steel dishes, because they're easy to clean and can't be demolished by a teething puppy.

Ceramic dishes are equally easy to clean and impervious to chewing. They also have the added advantage of weight, which keeps them from being knocked over. However, imported ceramic bowls — especially those that come from Central America — may contain lead, which can be toxic to dogs as well as to people. A prudent owner will stick with ceramic dishes manufactured in the United States.

Plastic dishes are convenient, cheap, and easy to clean, but may cause some dogs to lose their nose pigment. In addition, plastic dishes aren't as durable as stainless steel or ceramic.

Dogs with Eating Issues

Even though you've followed all the rules when feeding your dog, he may still not be the most consistent eater. The fact is, some dogs have eating issues — but you can help them deal with those issues. Here are some profiles of dogs with less-than-terrific eating habits, and some ideas on how to ease their dining difficulties.

The Fussy Eater

Some dogs can't seem to allow eating to be a simple act. They pick at and fuss with their food, walk away from it for a little while, and then come back to shove their food around in their dishes a little more. Some will take a little food out of the dishes and place it on the floor. Most leave food in their dishes when mealtime is supposed to be over.

Fussy eating has many causes. Some canine culinary fussbudgets may be getting too much to eat. Others don't like the way their food tastes or may even be bored with their fare. Still others may not feel well. Here's how to find out what's making your pooch so picky, and what to do once you do figure out what's going on.

✔ **Cut the serving size.** Your four-legged friend simply may not be as hungry as you think he is. If your dog is shoving his food around his dish and only eating two-thirds of it, try cutting his rations by a third or so at his next meal. You may find that he'll eat all his food, and do so a little more quickly.

✔ **Add a little something.** Some dogs who eat nothing but kibble may start picking at it after awhile, apparently bored with such monotonous fare. Consider adding some canned food to the kibble, and you may see his interest in eating perk up.

If your dog is turning up his nose at a canned-food-and-kibble combo, consider putting a nutritious little extra in his rations, such as finely chopped raw carrot, broccoli, Brussels sprouts, or beets. Many dogs enjoy vegetables, and a little bit of green or yellow veggie garnish could be all that's needed to jump-start your dog's appetite.

✔ **Nuke it.** Many dogs don't enjoy eating cold food. A quick turn in the microwave will give your dog's meal enough heat to release aromas that are bound to pique his interest — and the meal may taste better to him, too.

✔ **Change his food.** It's possible that your dog just doesn't like the food he's being offered. Consider *gradually* changing his rations to another brand or regimen and see whether that makes a difference.

✔ **Respect his dining preferences.** Some dogs, like my Cory, have definite ideas about the ideal dining environment. See whether your dog eats a little better if you stick around, minimize distractions, or do something else to subtly alter the conditions under which he eats.

✔ **Don't force the issue.** If your normally good eater picks at his food for one meal, don't try to coax or force him to eat. A normally healthy eater who suddenly shows a lack of interest in food may have an upset stomach. Any effort to force him to eat despite that stomach upset can result in vomiting soon after the meal.

✔ **Heed the warning.** A normal eater who skips or fusses at more than one consecutive meal could well be sick. Put in a call to your veterinarian — especially if your friend's diminished appetite is accompanied by other symptoms.

The Overeater

If your dog appears to live to eat rather than eat to live, he's got lots of company. Some veterinarians estimate that as many as half the dogs they treat are overweight.

Carting around too many pounds is just as bad for pooches as it is for people. Excess weight in dogs can trigger serious health problems, such as heart disease, diabetes, and arthritis. The extra poundage can also strain a dog's muscles, joints, and bones.

Sometimes, a dog's excess weight and overactive appetite signal an underlying problem, such as Cushing's disease (overproduction of adrenal hormone) or hypothyroidism (insufficient thyroid hormone production). Only a veterinarian can diagnose and treat such conditions, though, so a stop at your vet should be your first step in helping a pudgy pooch pare off some poundage.

More often, though, the reason that pooches pork out is the same as for people: too much food and too little exercise. Here's how you can help your dog shed some unneeded weight:

✔ **Talk with your vet.** Your veterinarian can help you map out a weight loss plan for your dog. Ask how many calories Fido needs to reach and maintain his ideal weight, and how much to reduce his current food rations to stay under that calorie quota.

✔ **Add some veggies.** If your dog seems to inhale his daily rations but still comes looking for more, veggies can help fill him up without adding calories. Brussels sprouts, green beans, carrots, and lettuce are all good options. And don't forget the fruit; for example, many dogs enjoy apples. Be aware, though, that adding vegetables to your dog's diet may cause him to need more bathroom breaks. Veggies contain fiber, which acts as a laxative.

✔ **Switch to low-cal food.** A low-calorie dog food also can fill up your friend without adding unnecessary calories. Again, though, be prepared to take your dog to the potty more often: low-cal dog foods contain extra fiber. And make the switch gradually; a sudden change in your dog's diet can trigger stomach upsets.

✔ **Ban free feeding.** Dogs with appetites on overdrive will eat whatever is put in front of them — so for these canines, free feeding is an especially bad idea. Don't keep your dog's dish full all day. Instead, feed him on a schedule and keep his dish empty at all other times.

✔ **Double the feedings.** Smaller, more frequent meals can boost a dog's metabolism and help him burn off calories more quickly. So, if you're feeding your dog only once a day, try splitting his daily ration into two meals.

✔ **Watch those treats.** Some table scraps and commercial pet treats are loaded with calories. Feeding them to your dog can undo all your efforts to cut his food intake. Instead, consider giving your four-legged friend frozen vegetables for between-meal snacks.

✔ **Get him moving.** Exercise is as good for dogs as it is for their people, especially if one or both are dieting. Try walking your portly pooch more often. And, if you can, give him opportunities to go swimming. A water workout will burn up lots of calories without putting excessive stress on your overweight dog's bones and joints.

The Beggar

The Beggar is the dog who attempts to guilt you out of the meal that you're eating. He sits and stares at you with big, soulful eyes that appear to plead with you to drop one, just one, morsel of food for poor li'l ol' him. A shy Beggar will sit some distance away from you while fixing you with what he hopes is a persuasive gaze. A bolder Beggar will sit as close to you as possible — and, if you don't get the message, nudge you with his nose.

Unfortunately, the Beggar generally doesn't learn this behavior all by himself. Instead, one or more humans in his family probably teach him that begging gets him what he wants — although they probably didn't intend to do so. Slipping Fido a morsel of hamburger while you're at the table, or letting a little piece of Thanksgiving turkey drop to the floor while you're carving it up, teaches Fido that if he hangs around long enough — and stares at you long enough — he'll score a tasty tidbit.

No matter what, though, begging shouldn't be tolerated. For one thing, it's obnoxious. For another, the extra goodies can turn your canine companion into an overly pudgy pooch. And finally, it's all too easy to slip Fido something that's not good for him such as cheese, which can induce a serious digestive ailment such as pancreatitis, or chocolate, which can actually kill a dog.

The best way to stop a Beggar is to not create one in the first place. In other words, don't give your dogs any unauthorized goodies from the table or the kitchen counter. Make sure that Fido's food dish is the one and only place from which he gets any food.

If you're already got a Beggar on your hands, though, here's how to put a stop to his behavior:

✔ **Feed him first.** Your dog's soulful stares may simply be his way of trying to tell you that he's hungry. If you keep European dinner hours — in other words, if you like eating relatively late in the evening — and your four-legged friend is still waiting for his grub, he may well be famished. Try feeding him before you feed yourself. You may find that once his tummy is full, he sleeps through your dinner instead of trying to get some of it.

✔ **Ignore him.** Tell yourself that you're not going to let your Beggar's soulful looks intimidate you. Pay absolutely no attention to any nudging or other hints that your Beggar bestows. And tell anyone else who dines in your house to do the same.

✔ **Banish him.** If you just can't stand those pleading looks — or if the other humans in the household are starting to weaken — put Fido someplace where he can't inflict his soulful stare upon you. One good place to put a relentless Beggar is in his crate. Be careful, though, to make it clear that the crate isn't a punishment. When you escort your Beggar to his doggie den, make sure that you put a treat or favorite toy in with him, so that he can enjoy himself while you enjoy your meal.

✔ **Get everyone onboard.** Your own efforts to stop your Beggar's behavior will be useless unless everyone in the household — including guests — agrees to do the same. In other words, make sure that no one in your pack gives your pleading pooch unauthorized goodies.

The Food Thief

That plate of ice cream you left out to soften — where could it be? And those hors d'oeuvres you were preparing for the evening's dinner guests — did they suddenly just vanish?

If you have a dog and you left those goodies unattended, the answer probably is no. And if you take a closer look at your dog, you'll probably see telltale bits of ice cream or crudités around his lips. Yup, your dog scarfed those goodies. You've got a genuine Food Thief.

Food thievery is no laughing matter. A dog who swipes the family grub not only risks his people's ire, but also jeopardizes the tranquility of his own tummy. The rich or spicy foods that some human beings favor can wreak havoc with a dog's digestive tract. And, all too often, a dog whose gut is on overdrive soon becomes a dog whose bowels are on overdrive, too — bad news for any housetraining effort.

Some experts suggest that people foil their canine Food Thief by creating a situation in which the dog tries to grab some unauthorized grub, but instead encounters something unpleasant, such as popping balloons or a hiding human with a squirt gun. But I think such measures are unfair to the dog. Food left within swiping range is just too much of a temptation for any dog to surmount.

The bottom line here is that if you don't want your dog to be a Food Thief, you shouldn't give him a chance to develop his thievery skills. In other words, don't leave unattended food within your four-legged friend's reach.

The Dog Who Eats the Wrong Things

Some dogs, alas, like eating things that aren't considered to be parts of normal diets. Instead of dining on meat, grains, and veggies, these dogs choose to chow on stuff like dirt, wood, sand, and stone. Experts call this unusual preference *pica.*

Experts used to think that the pooch with pica was suffering from a nutritional deficiency. Today, though, they're starting to consider pica to be a behavioral problem. Either way, pica can be hazardous to a dog's physical health. Ingested wood can splinter and cause internal injuries, while gobbled-up socks and stones may create blockages in the digestive tract that require emergency surgery.

Ultimately, help for the pooch with pica requires the help of an expert. If you see your dog consistently choosing to eat nonfood items, bring him to your veterinarian. Your vet and/or an animal behaviorist can suggest possible remedies, including medications, that can curb your canine's compulsion.

Part V
The Part of Tens

The 5th Wave   By Rich Tennant

"Down Skippy, down!! Mike has tried so hard to socialize this dog so we can have people over without being embarrassed, but evidently he needs a few more lessons."

In this part . . .

Sometimes housetraining poses more of a challenge than you anticipated. The challenge could result from mistakes you make in teaching toileting tactics, issues your dog has with bathroom matters, or something as simple as the possibility that your pooch is sick. Here, you get some ideas on how to deal with any and all bathroom issues that you or your canine companion has — as well as a guide to some of the best housetraining information in cyberspace.

Chapter 13

Ten Mistakes You Don't Have to Make

*H*ousetraining a puppy or dog can be a real challenge. A well-meaning but unprepared person can find plenty of opportunities to mess up the job while he attempts to achieve housetraining success. Some of these mistakes result from owner misunderstanding, while others occur due to owner impatience. However, any of these mistakes can make your canine companion's housetraining learning curve a lot steeper than it needs to be.

In fact, just about all housetraining mistakes are avoidable — if you know ahead of time what the possible pitfalls are. This chapter describes ten common housetraining booboos, why they occur, and how you can avoid making them.

Thinking the Crate Is Cruel

If your love for dogs began when you started watching TV shows such as *Lassie* when you were a kid, the idea of putting your dog in a crate probably takes a little bit of getting used to. The image of Timmy and his glorious collie wandering over rolling hills of farm land just doesn't square with the idea of confining your Fido in a plastic or wire enclosure until he learns his potty manners. In fact, you may feel that in doing so, you're putting Fido in a cage. "Dogs don't belong in cages," you may protest. "It's cruel."

But if Fido could speak for himself, he'd probably disagree with you.

That's because many dogs actually love their crates. To most of our canine companions, the crate is the safe, secure den they instinctively long for. The crate-den offers protection from hazards such as out-of-control children and big, noisy vacuum cleaners. It also makes a terrific home away from home for the traveling canine. For most dogs, then, the crate is not an object of cruelty, but an object to be appreciated.

And for people who love those dogs, the crate can be a dandy house-training tool. That's because when a dog is in her crate, her instinctive desire to keep her den clean kicks into gear. She won't eliminate in her crate if she can possibly avoid doing so. She'll hold her pee or poop until she can leave the crate.

Consequently, using a crate for housetraining just prompts a dog to do — or rather, not doo — what comes naturally. When you confine your canine-in-housetraining to a crate during those times that you can't watch her, you tap into her inborn desire to refrain from eliminating in the den. That helps her develop bowel and bladder control. Meanwhile, she's happy and secure while lounging in her beloved den. It's a classic win-win situation — about as far from cruelty as one can get.

Some dogs do take awhile to appreciate their crates. A very gradual introduction can help such a pooch discover the joys of chilling out in this makeshift den. Start by just letting him explore an open crate. Then try putting him in his crate with the door shut for just a few seconds. Gradually increase the time your dog spends there and try leaving the room for brief periods of time. Eventually your crate-phobic pooch should become a crate-loving canine — especially if you sweeten his crate stay with the addition of a tasty treat or a favorite toy.

There is one instance where being in the crate can be cruel to a dog, though: if he's left in there for too long. Don't leave your dog in his crate all day while you're at work. If you're concerned about destructiveness, enclose him in a dog-proofed room, hire someone to come walk him during the day, or take him to doggie day care.

Getting a Crate That's Too Big

This mistake is common among people who have acquired young puppies and are hoping to economize on their crates. Such individuals buy a crate that's sized for an adult dog, not a little canine youngster. The idea is that the puppy will have plenty of room to grow into her crate, and the owner will only have to shell out for a crate once. Unfortunately, the puppy not only has plenty of room to grow — he's also got enough room to sleep at one end of the crate and eliminate at the other. That defeats the purpose of the crate, which is to help the puppy develop bowel and bladder control. When that happens, the puppy's owner may well decide that a crate doesn't help a pooch to acquire good bathroom manners.

A crate that's too big is a little bit like a brassiere that's too big. Any woman will find that a loose bra is very comfortable, but she'll also discover that such an undergarment fails to fulfill its intended purpose: providing support where she needs it. Similarly, a too-big crate is certainly comfortable for a puppy, but it doesn't represent the cozy den he needs to learn to control his pooping and peeing.

The solution to this problem is to buy the correctly sized crate. A crate is sized correctly when it is just big enough for a dog to stand up, turn around, and lie down.

Does this mean that a new-puppy owner must run up his credit card balance by purchasing a new crate every time his puppy shows significant growth? Not at all! You can still get away with buying just one crate that fits little Fido's expected adult size. However, you also need to make that adult-sized crate smaller until little Fido is no longer little.

To cut an adult-sized crate down to puppy size, just block the puppy's access to the back half of the crate's interior. A cardboard crate divider, as described in Chapter 4, will fill the bill nicely. As your puppy grows, you can move the divider further and further toward the back of the crate, the same way you'd move a divider in a filing cabinet. That way, the crate will fulfill its purpose, but you'll only have to buy one once.

Failing to Stick to the Schedule

Normally you take your juvenile housetrainee out every day at lunchtime, but today you forgot. Or maybe you decided to stop off at the local watering hole after work, even though your housetrained canine companion was sitting home waiting for you to take her on a potty break.

Should you be surprised, then, to find a little puddle or pile greeting you when you do finally remember to take Fido out?

Your answer, on both counts, should be "No."

For the puppy or dog who's still being housetrained, sticking to the schedule is crucial to achieving success. That's because once you establish a schedule, your puppy will expect to eat, drink, and eliminate at certain times. That expectation helps you to anticipate when she needs to go and thus reduces the number of accidents she has. But it also helps her to develop enough bowel and bladder control to keep herself from eliminating until it's time for the potty break she's come to expect.

If she doesn't get that break, though, she may not be able to hold her water (or the other stuff). She may pass her personal point of endurance and have no choice but to unload.

That may also be true of the housetraining graduate. No dog can keep his floodgates shut forever. If you expect your dog to refrain from eliminating during the day, you can't reasonably expect him to continue to refrain during the evening. The next time you're tempted to stop off someplace else before going home to take your dog out, ask yourself this: Could I hold it as long as Fido has been holding it today? If the answer is no, high-tail it home and give your friend his break.

Bottom line: Do your very best to stick to the schedule you've created. You and Fido will both be glad you did.

Failing to Clean Up

Maybe you meant to clean up Fido's bathroom booboo of several hours ago. But while you were getting the pet stain cleaner, the phone rang, or your toddler climbed on top of the kitchen counter, or your washing machine overflowed. Now, to your horror, Fido's standing atop the scene of his earlier mistake, poised to pee a second time.

Or maybe you did try to clean up the booboo, but not with a commercial cleaner. Perhaps you'd used up your supply, and Fido took a whiz on the living room carpet before you had a chance to get a new bottle. Consequently, you grabbed the club soda in the fridge or the ammonia underneath your kitchen sink and used those to try to get rid of the stain. Unfortunately, Fido has returned to the scene of his crime and is clearly about to repeat his performance.

Clearly something is wrong, but not with Fido. What's at fault here is your clean-up technique.

In the first instance, the failure to clean up Fido's puddle has left the rug with a message that practically screams out to Fido, "Come back and do it again!" Canine urine is a magnet to dogs — including the dog from whom the urine came. Even one stray drop can lure a dog to a given area and prompt him to pee there.

In the second instance, using club soda and/or ammonia might have appeared to get rid of the urine stain, but it certainly didn't get rid of the odor. That come-hither fragrance has worked its dubious magic on Fido, drawing him back to the scene of his potty crime. If you used ammonia, you've not only failed to get rid of the odor — you've actually intensified it. That's because ammonia smells a lot like urine to most dogs.

The solution to both scenarios is obvious: If your pooch makes a potty mistake, clean it up completely — and use a commercial cleaner that's expressly designed for the job. Otherwise, you may as well tell Fido it's okay to flunk Housetraining 101.

Failing to Change the Papers or Litter

No question, life sometimes feels like a never-ending to-do list. Understandably, you'd like nothing better than to pare that list down a little bit. But failing to change your indoor trainee's soiled newspapers or litter shouldn't be one of the tasks you skip.

Do you like using a dirty bathroom? Of course not. Chances are, even if the rest of your house looks like a hurricane swept through it, your bathroom is reasonably tidy. And even though you probably don't enjoy cleaning your toilet, you do it anyway — because the very thought of using a dirty john grosses you out.

Your dog feels the same way that you do. He does not like to use a dirty bathroom. The idea of pooping or peeing on soaked papers or in a dirty litterbox grosses *him* out. But because he can't change his papers or litter himself, he's left with only one other alternative to using the canine equivalent of a dirty toilet: He poops or pees someplace else. That solves the dirty-toilet problem for him, but represents a house-training setback for both of you.

Make sure that you change your indoor trainee's papers or litter as soon as possible after your pooch has used them. That way, he'll stay on track with housetraining.

Thinking Your Dog Looks Guilty

You're on your way home after a long day grappling with office politics and are looking forward to spending time with your cherished canine companion. But when you walk in the door, you see a telltale stain on your gorgeous Oriental rug. When you cast a baleful glance over to your now not-so-cherished companion, he seems to wilt in front of you: He folds his ears back, places his tail between his legs, and looks away from you.

"Aha!" you might think. "He knows he's been bad. He knows that he shouldn't have peed on my rug. He feels so guilty he can't even look at me."

Time out.

Your dog's failure to meet your gaze does *not* result from guilt. His low-hanging ears and tail do *not* reflect remorse. His body language does not reflect any feelings he has from peeing on your rug. Before you walked in the door, he was probably taking a nap and wasn't thinking at all about how the rug got that stinky yellow stain. Only when you sent that menacing glance his way did he realize that he might be in trouble. And he responded accordingly: with body language that says, "I don't know why you're upset, but I'll do anything it takes to make you feel better."

 In other words, dogs don't know the meaning of guilt. Your dog has no idea that you're angry because he used your Oriental rug as a potty. He doesn't even remember having done so. He understands only that you're unhappy, and he's responding in the only way that he knows how.

Understanding that your dog doesn't feel guilty over his housetraining lapse means that you can't blame him for that lapse. If you yell at him, restrict him, or try to correct him for producing that puddle, he won't have the faintest idea why you're acting that way. He'll learn nothing from your rant, except to be afraid of you.

So instead of ranting at your dog when you're confronted with a house-training lapse, ask yourself how you could have prevented the lapse in the first place. And while you're asking, clean up the puddle and stain with a good commercial cleaner that's expressly designed for that purpose.

Rubbing His Nose in You-Know-What

Back in days of yore, people thought they could correct a dog for housetraining lapses no matter how long ago those lapses occurred. Many of those same people also thought that rubbing the offending pooch's nose in his poop or pee would further help him understand that doing his biz in the house was not a good thing to do.

But that really isn't the case. Giving the dog a snoutful of dog doo falls in the same category as thinking a dog looks guilty. Either way, dogs don't remember their housetraining mistakes. They don't feel bad for doing what comes naturally. And they don't connect having to eyeball their waste with having deposited that waste in the wrong place a few minutes or hours earlier.

 If you come upon a puddle or pile inside your house, it's too late to do anything but clean it up. Do that, resolve to prevent future accidents, and consign the nose-rubbing routine to where it belongs: the past.

Cleaning Up in Front of an Audience

Perhaps you believe that if your dog sees you clean up his unauthorized puddle or pile and realizes how angry you are, he'll wise up and never make a bathroom mistake again.

Dogs are wise, no doubt about it. Tales of their sagacity (not to mention their other admirable attributes) have filled more than a few books and made some authors rich in the process. However, watching their human friends clean up their bathroom booboos does not appear to develop canine wisdom.

In fact, some expert trainers believe that allowing your dog to watch you clean up is a very bad idea. They believe that doing so might give your dog the idea that you are her personal maid. I don't necessarily subscribe to that notion. But I do believe that having your dog witness your clean-up efforts does nothing to help him understand where he should and shouldn't potty. Moreover, it's possible that you could become so absorbed in your clean-up efforts that you fail to see Fido sneak off and have another accident someplace else.

Before you remove the evidence of your dog's latest bathroom setback, make sure that he doesn't have a chance to have another setback someplace else. At these times, the best place for him to be is his crate.

Changing the Menu Abruptly

You've been feeding Fido pretty much the same thing day in, day out for the past few weeks, and his housetraining's been coming along beautifully. In fact, you can't quite remember the last time you had to clean up a canine potty mistake.

Then, lo and behold, it's time to celebrate Thanksgiving or another holiday that calls for a grand and glorious feast for the human members of the family. But as you're preparing that feast, the nonhuman member of the family lays an incredibly effective guilt trip on you. As you baste that turkey or prepare that sausage stuffing, Fido's there with you, staring at you and the food with big, hungry eyes. And you ask yourself how you can possibly stuff yourself with such wonderful fare but force Fido to stick with kibble. You think, "What the heck" and decide to give Fido a Thanksgiving dinner, too. And he loves it. He practically inhales it.

Unfortunately, several hours later, Fido has a loose, runny bowel movement all over your floor or carpet. Your tender-hearted gesture at dinnertime has given Fido an exceptionally tender tummy now — and with all-too-predictable results.

Anytime you change a dog's menu suddenly, you risk upsetting his digestive system. Digestive upsets in dogs manifest themselves the same way as they do for people: with diarrhea.

Does this mean that Fido shouldn't enjoy Thanksgiving dinner along with the rest of the family? No! It does mean, though, that giving Fido a completely different meal all at once is likely to wreak havoc with his bathroom behavior. Let him have a little taste of the turkey (white meat, no skin). That way, he'll get to enjoy some holiday fare, without having to pay for it afterward.

The same principle applies when you're switching Fido's everyday fare. If you're changing dog foods or switching from commercial to home-cooked meals, don't make the change all at once. Do so over a period of several days, so that Fido's digestive system can become accustomed to the new grub. By taking your time with any culinary changes, you'll greatly reduce the risk of messy digestive upsets.

Declaring Victory Prematurely

Oh, you are *so* proud of your little Fifi, aren't you? She's been with you for only a month, she's just three months old, and she hasn't had an accident for a whole week. Surely she's a housetraining prodigy. How many other dogs her age have aced their bathroom lessons so quickly and so thoroughly?

Probably not many — including Fifi.

When it comes to housetraining, it's a big mistake to declare victory prematurely. It takes longer than a week, particularly with a puppy, to be sure that those potty lessons are imprinted onto the canine brain. For one thing, a three-month-old puppy doesn't have enough physical bowel and bladder control to be considered reliable for long periods of time. Even adult dogs who *have* developed that control may have trouble remembering where and when they're supposed to potty.

With canine children as well as with human children, it's better not give too much freedom too soon. The parents of a five-year-old child who's learned to ride a two-wheeled bike aren't likely to let that child ride the bike alone to the other side of town — at least not right away. Similarly, your canine child's housetraining prowess does not merit unsupervised access to the whole house. Give her longer stretches of unsupervised time outside her crate, or try taking her out a little less often. With both kids and puppies, gradually increased privileges get better results than total immediate freedom.

Chapter 14

Ten Problem Potty-ers and How to Help Them

In This Chapter

▶ Describing dogs with bathroom issues

▶ Solving common housetraining problems

. . . .

*A*lmost every dog has housetraining problems at one time or another. Some pooches have trouble mastering their bathroom basics. Others ace Housetraining 101, but run into toilet trouble later.

Whether your dog's potty problems make him a slow learner or a conflicted canine, there's help at hand. Among the following profiles of dogs with housetraining issues is at least one that should shed some light on your housetrainee's particular problem and give you ideas about how to solve it.

The Dog Who Pees On Her Back

When you come home, does your canine companion fold her ears back, look away from you, and tuck her wagging tail between her legs? If you bend over to put the leash on her, does she roll onto her back? And does she dribble a little bit of urine at such times — whether lying on her back or standing on all fours?

If so, take heart. Your dog doesn't have a housetraining problem at all. The urine she dribbles does not indicate a lack of bathroom manners. Instead, she's trying to tell you that she worships the ground you walk on.

Dogs who look away from a person or another canine, tuck their tails between their legs, fold back their ears, and leak a little bit of urine are showing what experts call submissive behavior. In other words, they are willing to submit to the wishes of the more dominant individual.

The little puddle on the ground emphasizes this respect. And if the dog leaks this urine while lying on her back, she is being even more submissive. She is not — repeat, not — making a housetraining mistake.

You need to treat The Dog Who Pees on Her Back very gently. She's a highly sensitive individual who needs your help to gain a little bit more self-confidence, or at least time to collect herself so that she doesn't pee on your floor or carpet. Here are some ideas to help her — and rescue your floors:

- ✔ **Ignore her.** Yes, really. When you come home in the evening or at any other time after being away for a while, don't pay any attention to your ecstatic pooch, no matter how much she throws herself at you or tries to get your attention. By ignoring her and giving her a few minutes to calm down, you'll reduce the likelihood that she will dribble. After a few minutes, you should be able to say hello to her.

- ✔ **Play it cool.** When you do greet your dog, don't make a big deal of it. Say a quiet hello, smile at her, and maybe give her a little pat. Don't hug her, smooch her, coo to her, or do any excited baby talk to her, no matter how much you've missed her. Your objective here is to help her stay calm so that she doesn't pee.

- ✔ **Get down to her level.** Some submissive dogs start leaking when their human leaders stand over them — for example, to put on their leashes. If yours is such a pooch, try squatting or sitting on the floor so that your eyes are level with your dog's. By getting down to her level, you avoid giving your dog the message that you are the boss, and she is not. That message is what prompts her to pee in response. In effect, she's saying, "I know you're the boss, and I will do whatever you ask."

- ✔ **Don't look at her.** Other submissive dogs start dribbling when their special persons look directly into their eyes. That's because in dog-talk, a direct gaze or stare is considered a dominant, I'm-the-boss type of gesture — and a submissive dog will pee to show that she understands her lowly place in the pack hierarchy. But if you look away, she won't need to make that submissive response.

Some very submissive dogs may call for special handling. Years ago, I adopted a little mixed poodle named Molly who'd been abused by her previous owner. Molly was a very submissive dog and would greet my nightly homecomings by rolling onto her back and leaking urine onto my foyer floor. To help Molly collect herself, I would restrain myself from petting her or even talking to her when I came home. Instead, I would silently sit on the floor and wait for her to come to me. When she reached me, I would look away from her and attach the leash to her collar. After several months of this routine, Molly finally felt sufficiently calm and confident to hold her water when I came home from work at night.

The Dog Who Leaves His Mark

If you're seeing dribs and drabs of dog pee on vertical surfaces inside your home, your pooch probably doesn't have a housetraining problem. A more likely possibility is that he's dealing with turf issues.

That's because dogs pee not only because their bladders are full, but also because they want to communicate with other canines. Just about any dog will sniff the place where another dog took a whiz, and often the sniffer will decide to pee on the same spot. However, an intact male dog may lift his leg and direct a little jet stream onto vertical surfaces so that he can announce that those surfaces are part of his domain. In other words, such a dog uses his pee to mark his territory.

A turf-conscious dog generally sends his messages to other canines, but some canines also try to send such messages to people. Years ago, when I was staying at a friend's country home for the first time, I awoke during the middle of one night just in time to see my friend's dog lift his leg and anoint the corner of the bed I was sleeping in. The dog's message was clear: I was an interloper, and he didn't appreciate my presence.

Dealing successfully with The Dog Who Leaves His Mark requires several actions. Here's what you should do:

- ✔ **Neuter him.** Your canine guy will be much less concerned about whose turf is where if he's not at the mercy of his raging canine male hormones. Make sure, too, that any other animals in the house also are spayed or neutered.

- ✔ **Keep it clean.** Make sure that you thoroughly clean any area that your dog has anointed. Otherwise, the smell of the previous dousing will bring him to the same spot for an encore performance.

  Check out Chapter 6 for information on effective indoor cleaners.

- ✔ **Start remedial housetraining.** Set up a housetraining routine such as the one described in Chapter 8 or 9 and follow it religiously until your dog confines his peeing to the papers, litterbox, or outdoors.

- ✔ **Catch him in the act.** If you see your dog start to lift his leg and/or anoint a surface, distract him by clapping your hands or making some other loud noise. Then, get him to his potty area as soon as possible.

- ✔ **Take him to school.** If you haven't done so already, find an obedience class for your dog. By learning how to teach him maneuvers such as coming when called, sitting, and lying down, you'll make it clear to your dog that you are the boss, and that he has no business telling you whose turf is whose.

✔ **Build a peaceable kingdom.** If your dog is marking his turf because there's an unfamiliar human guest in the house, show your canine companion that he's got nothing to worry about. Have the guest play with or feed the dog. Once Fido realizes that the guest is a friend rather than a threat, the marking behavior may stop.

On the other hand, perhaps your dog is displaying his marksmanship to establish his place among the other four-legged members of your household. If that's the case, try to resolve any conflicts between the marker and your other pets. Feed them separately from each other — at different times and/or in different locations — and try to give each animal equal amounts of affection.

✔ **Ask for help.** Canine marking behavior can be difficult to eliminate. If your dog persists in christening unauthorized areas, ask your vet for a referral to a qualified trainer or animal behaviorist.

The Fussbudget

Some dogs are very particular about where they choose to potty. They'll investigate this spot, then that one, and yet another one, in what all too often seems like an endless quest to find the perfect place to pee. They are incredibly fussy about where they will do their business, which is why I dub such a dog the Fussbudget.

To his credit, the Fussbudget has learned his housetraining lessons well. To his detriment — and to your frustration — he may have learned his lessons a little too well. When it's raining cats and dogs (so to speak), or when the temperature is so cold that icicles are forming in your mustache, or it's late at night and you're bone-tired, the last thing you want to deal with is a dog who delays doing his duty. You want him to take that whiz *now*.

The best way to deal with the often nervous, frequently uptight Fussbudget is to force yourself to chill out and then find ways to help him chill as well. The best help you can give him is to show him other places to potty. For example, if you can remember another place where he's recently peed, try taking him there again. Once he's there, he may smell his previous anointing. The odor may jog his memory and prompt him to repeat his performance.

Another similar tack is to take the Fussbudget to a place where you know other dogs have done their business. Most dogs, when confronted with other canine calling cards, feel compelled to leave some of their own.

The One-Bathroom Dog

The One-Bathroom Dog is really the ultimate Fussbudget: He will potty only in one particular place. If he cannot reach this particular location, he will just not do his duty. He'll attempt to hold his water for as long as it takes for his people to get him back to his chosen bathroom location.

Many people don't initially perceive the disadvantage of having a One-Bathroom Dog. That's because these set-in-their-ways canines potty like clockwork when taken to their designated areas. The disadvantage becomes apparent only when the One-Bathroom Dog is away from home. Whether he's staying overnight at the vet's or is making a rest stop on the highway while traveling with his human companion, this pooch just won't potty unless he's in his own "bathroom."

Some One-Bathroom Dogs may respond to the same tactics that work with the Fussbudget, particularly taking them to a place where other dogs have done their business. For other such pooches, though, the communal potty remedy may not do the trick. A better bet for these stubborn dogs is to find a way to take that single bathroom with them wherever they go. The best porta-potty comes in the form of the same device you may have used to housetrain your dog in the first place: the pre-scented cloth. Here's how to pre-scent a cloth and use it.

1. **Bring your dog to his usual toilet area and let him take a whiz.**

2. **After he does his duty, gently wipe his urinary area or the ground he's anointed with the paper towel.**

3. **Pack the paper towel in a plastic bag and have it ready when the two of you make a roadside pit stop or otherwise need to use an unfamiliar bathroom.**

4. **When you make that stop, place the paper towel at the place on the ground where you want him to go.**

   Chances are, he'll do just that.

The Bedwetter

Although dogs generally will do just about anything to avoid peeing in the places where they sleep, some pooches do wet their beds. However, such behavior is not normal, and you should not treat it as such.

The bad news here is that a dog who wets her bed is invariably a dog with a medical problem; she needs to see a veterinarian as soon as possible. The good news is that the canine Bedwetter's problem is generally not serious and almost always is very treatable.

Among the dogs most likely to leak urine in their sleep are older spayed females. Just as older human females tend to have more trouble holding their water than is the case with their younger sisters, so is the case with older canine females. For the latter, veterinarians often prescribe a short course of diethylstilbestrol, better known as DES. This synthetic compound has the properties of natural estrogens and can help a dowager doggie stay dry all night long.

If you are pregnant — or are trying to become pregnant — do not administer DES to your bedwetting female dog. Have someone else do it. DES has been known to cause miscarriages, birth defects, and long-term problems among human babies.

Male dogs who wet their beds at night may be suffering from urinary tract infections or kidney infections. They, too, need veterinary treatment. In most cases, the vet will ask you to bring a urine sample, and will prescribe a week to ten days of antibiotics.

The Teensy-Weensy Dog

As a pet journalist, I've written my share of dog breed profiles for magazines and Web sites. One thing that's always struck me is that whenever I'm writing about a very small dog, such as a Chihuahua or Shih Tzu, the experts I interview invariably tell me that these pint-sized pooches have big-sized housetraining problems. Basically, the little guys and gals flunk Housetraining 101.

Why does this happen? Are tiny dogs' bladders too small to hold their pee? Are they intellectually incapable of learning proper potty deportment? Or is this apparent failure really the fault of their human teachers?

Most experts agree that it's the people, not the pooches, who are at fault here. People who live with teensy-weensy dogs just find them to be so cute that they aren't as vigilant about housetraining as people who have larger dogs. Compounding the problem is the fact that *les petit chiens* make much smaller puddles than their bigger brethren do. Consequently, those puddles are far easier to overlook than the larger ponds and lakes that emerge from bigger dogs.

When it comes to housetraining, size doesn't matter. No matter how big or little the pooch is, you shouldn't let them pee or poop wherever they choose. All canine bodily waste smells bad, stains carpets and floors, and contains bacteria that make both dogs and people sick. Consequently, housetraining is just as important for little dogs as for big ones. Don't let your pint-sized pooch's cuteness get in the way of his learning his bathroom basics. He's just as capable of acing his housetraining lessons as the big dogs are. All he needs is consistent, patient guidance from you.

The Canine Hottie

Is your female dog licking her "private parts" a lot? Do they look swollen? Is she bleeding from her vaginal area?

If the answer to any of those questions is yes, your dog doesn't have a housetraining problem. In fact, she's probably just fine. In fact, she's showing her canine womanhood.

That's right: Your dog is experiencing something like the canine equivalent of a human menstrual period, but there's a significant difference between the two. A human female's menstrual period generally signals that she is not pregnant. A canine female's menstrual period — more commonly known as her heat cycle — means that she can become pregnant if she mates with a male dog within about a week.

To deal with your female dog's bloody discharge, get her some doggie diapers, which are available at most pet supply stores.

More important, though, is the need to keep your dog away from any and all male dogs if you do not want her to have puppies. Once her heat cycle is over, which will be about three weeks after the first bloody discharge begins, have her spayed. That way, you'll never again need to deal with heat cycles, overexcited male dogs, or the possibility that she could become pregnant unexpectedly. You'll also make an important contribution to eliminating the problem of pet overpopulation.

The Poop Eater

Some dogs, alas, are not content to eat the food that we prepare for them. They choose to eat other items as well, ranging from the merely bizarre to the out-and-out disgusting. In the latter category is that truly gross practice that experts call *coprophagy,* but which the rest of us call poop eating or stool eating.

No one really knows why a Poop Eater indulges in this pastime. Although some experts have speculated that a dog who eats stool suffers from sort of nutritional deficiency, this belief hasn't been proven. Others believe that the habit may result from anxiety or stress, particularly among dogs who spend a lot of time in kennels.

The best way to deal with a Poop Eater is to keep him from getting to the poop in the first place. Walk your dog on a leash outdoors, so that you can keep him away from any poop lying on the ground. Better yet, don't leave any poop on the ground. Clean it up right away.

The Dog Who Gets Distracted

Does your four-legged friend seem more interested in chasing off any squirrels who invade your backyard than in doing her business there? Does she pick up a stick for you to throw if you enter the yard? If you take her for a walk, is she more likely to bark at the dog ambling on the other side of the street than to poop or pee? In other words, when it's time for your pooch to potty, does pottying appear to be the last thing she wants to do?

If so, you've got a Dog Who Gets Distracted. To bring her attention back to her job — to poop or pee — you need to take on the job of minimizing distractions. If your dog gets sidetracked while out in the yard, consider walking her on the leash to her potty area until she remembers why she's supposed to be out there. If her lack of focus occurs while you're out walking her, take steps to regain her attention: For example, try turning around and walking in the opposite direction.

Also consider adjusting your pooch's bathroom schedule. Your dog may be uninterested in doing her duty simply because she doesn't have to go — especially if she's an older puppy who's still on a younger puppy's schedule. If your distractible friend is over five months of age but you're still taking her out every couple of hours, give yourself a break. Let her hold her water longer, and she'll probably do her duty more promptly when you do take her out.

The Dog Who Gets Amnesia

Sometimes an impeccably housetrained dog seems to suddenly forget his bathroom manners. He may pee inside the house soon after returning from a trip to his outdoor potty. He may poop or pee in front of his human companion without having asked to go out.

If your dog appears to suffer from housetraining amnesia, and if he's more than seven years of age, he may suffer from a condition called *canine cognitive dysfunction syndrome,* or CDS. The condition is very similar to human Alzheimer's disease. In addition to the loss of housetraining skills, dogs with CDS may be disoriented, appear to no longer recognize the other members of the family, and sleep more during the day but less during the night.

Any elderly dog who exhibits symptoms of CDS should be seen by a veterinarian. The vet will examine your canine companion and order lab tests that can identify other possible causes of housetraining and other problems, such as kidney or liver disease. If those causes are eliminated, a CDS diagnosis is likely.

CDS isn't curable, but medication can slow its progress and alleviate some of its symptoms, including housetraining amnesia.

Chapter 15

Ten Potty Problems That May Mean Your Dog Is Sick

In This Chapter

▶ Dealing with canine bathroom ailments

▶ Collecting potty samples

Some dogs develop potty problems that have nothing to do with their housetraining prowess. Instead, these apparent bathroom lapses may actually signal that Fido's not feeling well. Some bathroom-symptom illnesses are minor; others are more serious and can even be life-threatening. Unfortunately, though, most people with pooches can't tell which is which.

That's why you should take your dog to the veterinarian for a checkup any time he appears to have forgotten his bathroom manners. And in fact, most of the conditions I describe in this chapter require a veterinarian's attention. But you still have an important role to play in maintaining your dog's health. By observing your pooch's particular potty problem, you can provide your veterinarian valuable information that can lead to effective treatment sooner than might otherwise be the case.

The following list of potty-related ailments is not inclusive. Plenty of other maladies may exhibit symptoms that are similar or identical to those described here. The bottom line here: If your dog's bathroom behavior deviates significantly from what's normal for him, he could very well be sick. Put in a call to your veterinarian.

Constant Peeing

A housetrained dog who's suddenly peeing all over the house probably hasn't developed bathroom amnesia. And if she gets to her potty spot, but asks to go there every hour on the hour, her bladder hasn't suddenly shrunk. In both cases, she's probably developed a urinary tract infection, or UTI.

Although they're uncomfortable (ask any person who's gotten one!), UTIs aren't necessarily serious — if they're treated promptly. You can't doctor these infections yourself, though. Treatment begins with a visit to your veterinarian. She'll examine your dog, analyze a urine sample, and prescribe the antibiotics needed to knock out the infection.

The antibiotics will take several days to eliminate the UTI. In the meantime, though, here's what you can do to make your canine companion more comfortable:

✔ **Step up bathroom breaks.** A dog with a UTI who pees all the time is doing exactly what she needs to do: flushing the infectious bacteria out of her system. So to help your UTI-ridden friend help herself, let her take as many potty breaks as she needs. If your pooch potties outside, be prepared to let her out or take her to her potty area (or, if you won't be home, ask a neighbor to do so) every couple of hours or so. If your dog uses papers or a litterbox, make sure that its location is never more than a few steps from where she is.

✔ **Encourage her to drink.** To encourage those potty breaks, do what you can to persuade your pooch to drink as much water as possible. Start by keeping her water dish filled with fresh water. Another good idea is to place several water bowls in various areas of the house, so that your dog never needs to walk too far to get herself a drink.

✔ **Finish those meds.** Although a dog's UTI symptoms generally abate after just a couple of days on antibiotics, it's important to finish out the entire prescription, which generally runs a week to ten days. That's because even though the symptoms have subsided, the infection may still be present — and stopping the meds prematurely will allow it to worsen. When that happens, the symptoms return with a vengeance.

Constant Drinking . . . and Constant Peeing

A dog who suddenly starts drinking more water than usual (and, consequently, starts peeing more than usual) could be suffering from one of several conditions. Some of these conditions are serious, while others aren't. Here are just a few of the possible suspects:

✔ **Hot weather.** If your dog's water intake rises soon after the onset of a heat wave, you probably can blame the weather. During hot spells, a dog may drink more water than usual simply to maintain a normal body temperature.

✔ **Diabetes.** Diabetes in both dogs and people occurs when the pancreas either produces too little insulin, or poorly functioning insulin. Either way, the amount of sugar in the bloodstream rises, and the individual will drink more water in order to dilute the sugar. Diabetic dogs also may have ravenous appetites and often are overweight.

✔ **Kidney problems.** When a dog's kidneys aren't functioning well, he urinates much more often than usual and can't retain the fluids his body needs. Consequently, he tries to offset the loss by drinking more water, which in turn spurs still more peeing and fluid loss. Some kidney problems are simple infections that a vet can treat with antibiotics. Others are much more serious, though, involving permanent damage to the organ. Those types also require a vet's care and expertise.

✔ **Cushing's disease.** This condition occurs when a dog's body produces too much adrenal hormone. In addition to excessive drinking and urinating, a dog with Cushing's may also suffer from hair loss, a drooping abdomen, panting, increased appetite, and muscle weakness.

The problem with constant drinking and peeing is that only a veterinarian can perform the tests needed to diagnose and treat a dog with such symptoms. Bottom line: Get your canine companion to his doctor if he's suddenly starting to pee and drink more often.

Pee That Comes Out Slowly . . . Or Not At All

Some dogs may do their darndest to pee, only to have little to show for their efforts. They'll execute their pre-potty maneuvers, position themselves accordingly, and then release next to nothing. Maybe a drop or two will emerge, if that.

Such a dog is clearly straining to pee — and he needs to see a veterinarian right away. The reason: He may well have urinary stones, which can be fatal if left untreated.

Urinary stones form when minerals that usually pass from the dog's body when he pees clump together instead. Generally, these stones are located in the bladder, but sometimes they can move to the urethra, which leads from the bladder to the outside of the body. If a stone is large enough, it can become trapped in the urethra, restricting or even completely blocking the urinary flow. A total blockage can cause sudden kidney failure, which in turn can kill the dog.

To determine whether a dog has stones, a vet will palpate the abdomen, analyze a urine sample, and may x-ray or perform an ultrasound of the dog's abdomen. Once stones are discovered, though, treatment depends on the type of mineral that forms the stone. Some stones respond to medicines that change the urine's chemistry, while others need to be removed surgically.

If your vet tells you that your dog's stones are made of calcium oxalate, try substituting distilled water for the tap water your dog drinks. Unlike tap water, distilled water doesn't contain those minerals — and without minerals, stones can't form.

Odd-Looking Pee

A dog's pee should be yellow. Period. If at any time your canine companion's urine doesn't evoke thoughts of the late Frank Zappa's notorious ditty, "Don't Eat the Yellow Snow," you need to call your vet.

Dark-looking urine — either rust-colored or slightly red — signals the presence of blood. Bloody urine may result from a urinary tract infection or can signal some other internal injury. Either way, a trip to the vet is in order.

Very light-colored or clear urine, especially first thing in the morning, may mean that your dog's kidneys aren't retaining as much water for her body as they should be. Such a dog also may be peeing a lot and drinking more water than usual. Among the possible causes are kidney disease or Cushing's disease. Any way you look at it, though, your job is the same: getting your four-legged friend to her veterinarian as soon as possible.

Diarrhea, A.K.A. Poop on the Run

Dog poop should be firm and compact and shouldn't stink — at least not very much. All too often, though, a dog's poop not only smells bad, but also comes out fast, furious, and often. To make matters worse, it looks very runny. In other words, he's got "poop on the run," better known as diarrhea.

There are lots of reasons that a dog can get diarrhea. Some are serious and require a veterinarian's attention. Others aren't as big a deal and respond to home care.

Here's what you can do to help reduce the runs:

✔ **Forget about food** — at least for the next day or so. Your dog's digestive system, which has been working overtime, needs to take a breather. A 24-hour fast will give your canine companion's digestive tract the time it needs to calm down a little bit.

✔ **But don't forget the water.** Diarrhea can dehydrate a dog pretty quickly, because that runny poop leeches liquids from a dog's bodily systems. To forestall dehydration, keep fresh water available for your four-legged friend.

✔ **Start a bland diet.** After a day or so, start giving your dog some food that's easy on the tummy. A good foundation for a bland diet is a mixture of boiled rice and hamburger. Be sure to pour off any fat from the hamburger while it cooks; leaving in the grease can bring on a new round of the runs.

✔ **Know when to get help.** Most cases of diarrhea abate within a day or two. But if your dog's still got the runs after two days, put in a call to your veterinarian. If your dog is also vomiting and drinking a lot of water, call your vet sooner. In fact, young puppies with diarrhea who vomit more than once an hour over a half-day period or so should see a veterinarian immediately.

Poop That Comes Slowly — Or Not at All

If your dog's poop comes out very slowly, despite his best efforts to produce some, he may be constipated — in other words, he may have the opposite of diarrhea. But even though they're opposites, there's one way these two ailments are very much alike: Their presence can signal either a minor problem or a major ailment. The trick is to know which is which. Waiting for a little while — no more than a day — should result in an answer.

Meanwhile, though, try the following relief-producing measures for your anal-retentive friend:

✔ **Give him some veggies.** Many dogs enjoy getting some vegetables added to their daily rations — and this is one dietary preference that can be good for your canine companion. Vegetables such as carrots, green beans, broccoli, and beets provide the bulk needed to loosen up a puppy's poopmaker. In addition, they're low in calories, which makes them terrific treats for pudgy pooches.

✔ **Lay on the liquid.** Your dog needs water to stay healthy, and extra water can soften the stool that's packed inside your pooch. Keep your friend's water dish filled with fresh, cool water — and if he's still not drinking, try placing several water bowls throughout the house. To overcome the reluctance of Cory, my canine office-mate, to get himself a drink from the water dish that's upstairs in the kitchen when I'm downstairs in my office, I simply place a second water dish near the room where I'm working.

✔ **Get him moving.** Simple constipation often clears up with some extra exercise — as though additional movement on the outside gets a dog's insides going, too.

✔ **Know when to get help.** If your dog's symptoms don't clear up in a day or so, and he's clearly trying to take a dump, take him to your vet. He could be suffering from a bowel obstruction or other serious problem. If he begins to vomit, see your vet sooner.

Poop That Contains Other Things

Sometimes a dog's poop is more than just bodily waste. Even a cursory glance can reveal the presence of substances that are decidedly unpoopy. Those substances may be the result of dietary indiscretions by your dog or less-than-optimum food preparation by you. They can also signal the presence of unwanted critters in your dog's digestive system.

For example, if your dog's deposits look like they're laced with grains, sprouts, or pasta, he's probably got worms. A tapeworm infestation will show up in the stool as substances that look like little bits of rice. Roundworms, on the other hand, look like thin spaghetti or alfalfa sprouts. With either parasite, your vet can provide proper treatment.

Maybe, though, you're seeing bits of little plastic or threads in your dog's stool. If so, your buddy's probably eating his toys or some socks in addition to (or instead of) his usual fare. The remedy here is preventive: Make sure that your dog is playing with his toys, not chewing on them. Plastic toys with small parts can be especially dangerous, because your dog can choke on them. Socks may be equally hazardous, because they can cause a blockage in a dog's digestive tract.

And if your dog likes vegetables, you may find chunks of those vegetables in your pooch's poop. Dogs can't absorb the nutrients in vegetables unless they're chopped up to a very fine degree. The remedy here: Sharpen your veggie-chopping skills or haul out the food processor.

Soft, Stinky Poop

Is your dog's poop full of mucus? Is it really soft when you scoop it up? And does it stink to high heaven? If so, chances are your canine companion's got giardia, a protozoan parasite. Other symptoms of giardia may include diarrhea, diminished appetite, weight loss, and vomiting.

Veterinarians report that they're seeing more and more dogs with giardia, which usually is spread when a dog drinks contaminated water or walks through damp areas and licks his feet afterward.

 As with so many other bathroom maladies, getting rid of giardia requires a veterinarian's expertise. The most common remedy is an antibacterial drug called metronidazole, better known as Flagyl. However, you can help keep these unwelcome little critters at bay by following good sanitary practices such as washing your hands whenever you handle an infected animal. And, because giardia thrive in damp environments, keeping the dog's living area dry is a very good idea.

Gray, Greasy Poop

Is your dog's fecal output gray and greasy-looking? Has he had diarrhea for a long time, despite the efforts of you and your veterinarian to treat him? Is his coat thin-looking? Does he look malnourished?

 If so, your dog's problem may be his pancreas, an organ that produces not only the hormone insulin, but also special enzymes that help his body digest the nutrients in his food. Sometimes the pancreas doesn't produce enough of those enzymes, particularly those that break down the fat in foods. Consequently, the fat passes through the body and ends up in the poop, giving the stool that greasy look. A dog with this condition is suffering from *exocrine pancreatic insufficiency,* or EPI.

 Many cases of EPI can be treated by putting the dog on a lowfat diet and prescribing medicines that contain the digestive enzymes the dog can't produce. Of course, the key to diagnosing and managing this condition is — yup — to bring your dog to his veterinarian.

Black Poop

A dog with black or very dark brown poop may be bleeding from his stomach or elsewhere in his upper digestive tract. Such bleeding, particularly if the poop resembles wet coffee grounds, could indicate the presence of a tumor or an ulcer.

By contrast, if you see red blood in your dog's poop, he's probably suffering from irritation in his colon or rectum.

 Either way, the presence of blood in the stool indicates that a serious health problem may be afoot. A call and visit to your vet is in order.

Collecting potty samples

To figure out what may be causing a dog's potty problems, veterinarians need to analyze her bathroom output. Unfortunately, vets can't send their patients to the bathroom down the hall and ask them to pee into a cup, nor can they give them one of those stool smear sample cards to use. That means that you must find a way to collect the poop and pee samples that your veterinarian needs to help your four-legged friend.

However, these tasks needs not be daunting. To collect either urine or stool, all you need are an oblong plastic bag, such as the kinds that newspapers and bread loaves are wrapped in, and an airtight plastic container. Armed with your sampling equipment, proceed to collect your dog's urine as follows:

1. **Take your dog to her potty spot.**

2. **Pull the plastic bag over your hand and wrist.**

3. **Hold the container with your bagged hand.**

4. **Watch your dog carefully; as soon as she bends her knees or he lifts his leg, push the container into position with your bagged hand.**

   That way, any errant dog pee will splash on the bag rather than on you.

5. **Cover the container.**

6. **Remove the bag from your hand and put it in the trash.**

7. **Bring the container to your veterinarian as soon as possible.**

Collecting a dog's poop is even easier. Here's what you need to do:

1. **Put the plastic bag over your hand.**

2. **Take your dog to her potty spot.**

3. **Watch for signs that your dog's about to "do the doo" and then pick up the poop with your bagged hand after she's finished.**

4. **With the other hand, pull the bag inside out.**

   The poop will now be inside the bag, at the bottom.

5. **Knot the bag with your hand and take it to your veterinarian as soon as possible**

   If you want to, put it in an airtight container.

Chapter 16

Ten Helpful Pit Stops on the World Wide Web

*T*he World Wide Web has become a goldmine of information on just about every subject under the sun, including housetraining. Here's a sampling of Web sites that provides excellent guidance for canine potty trainees and their people — and a couple of excellent sites that appear to deal with bathroom matters, but really don't.

Dog Owner's Guide

This is one of the best dog-oriented sites on the Web. Created by long-time dog writer and animal activist Norma Bennett Woolf, the Dog Owner's Guide is chock-full of information for people who live with dogs. The site contains over 300 pages of features ranging from how to select a canine companion to reviews of the latest dog care books. Among those 300 pages are at least five on some aspect of housetraining.

www.canismajor.com/dog/guide.html

Wonder Puppy

The Wonder Puppy here is U-CDX Goldie's Lucky Leilah CGC WGP, a Vizsla/Pointer mix. Leilah's "mom," known to the cyber-world as Fran(oise, has put together a comprehensive multipage site that contains, among other things, nearly two dozen housetraining links. In addition to general housetraining information, Fran(oise has also included links to suggestions for cleaning up accidents, a list of housetraining myths and facts, a special section on teaching bathroom manners to puppy mill dogs, and recommendations for dealing with housetraining problems.

www.wonderpuppy.net

Denver Dumb Friends League

Of the many humane organizations and rescue groups that populate cyberspace, the Web site offered by Colorado's Denver Dumb Friends League is one of the best. The League was founded in 1910, a time when the term "dumb" was often used to refer to those who could not speak. And in fact, even today, the League's motto is that "We speak for those who cannot speak for themselves" — in other words, for animals.

Among the two-dozen-plus links to dog training topics are five that deal directly with housetraining issues: submissive urination, removing odors and stains, crate training, housetraining for puppies, and remedial housetraining for adult dogs.

www.ddfl.org

Rec.Pets.Dogs.Behavior FAQ

The mother of online dog information is the vast collection of breed, behavior, and other FAQs (frequently asked questions) maintained under the Rec.Pets.Dogs umbrella. The Rec.Pets.Dogs electronic news group predates the Web; its offshoots deal with health, behavior, and rescue topics, among other subjects. The 16-page behavior FAQ, authored by Cindy Tittle Moore, includes three devoted to solving common housetraining problems such as sudden lapses, poop eating, and submissive urination.

www.k9web.com/dog-faqs/behavior.html

Doglitter.com

This is the SecondNature Dog Litter Web site maintained by the manufacturer, Nestle-Purina. The inclusion of this site among my top ten cyber pit stops is not an endorsement of SecondNature over the other major litter that was on the market at the time this book was written. However, the site contains some good basic housetraining information that anyone can apply to potty-training a dog, regardless of the housetraining method used.

www.doglitter.com

Dogz-One Reading Room

A site targeted primarily to breeders, the Dogz-One Reading Room nevertheless contains some good basic information on housetraining and other subjects that both breeders and pet owners can learn from. If you're looking to lighten your day, check out the "Bad to the Home" link by Melody Underwood Hobbs.

www.dogzone.com/reading/reading.htm

American Dog Trainers Network

The late New York City dog trainer and writer Robin Kovary put together an impressive collection of articles about all aspects of dog ownership, including housetraining. In addition, Kovary — who was featured in a wide range of books, magazines, newspapers, and newsletters — started a trainer's telephone help line. People who are having housetraining or other behavioral problems with their pooches can obtain advice from an expert just for the price of a long-distance call.

www.canine.org

Pooper-Scooper

If cleaning up your dog's solid waste gives you the willies, or if your dog is pooping faster than you can clean up after him, you may want to head over to Matthew Osborn's professional pooper-scooper's Web site. Among its features are a worldwide directory of dog waste removal services, a message board, a FAQs section, and links to other dog-related Web sites. For the enterprising individual who thinks he can overcome his aversion to dog doo, there's also a link to an order form for Osborn's book on how to start a professional pooper-scooper service.

www.pooper-scooper.com

The Poop.com

This e-zine has very little to do with dog doo per se. It does, however, offer lots of articles on other aspects of family dog ownership. Included on the site are experts' answers to cyber-surfers' questions about dogs, links to rescue groups and adoption groups, message boards, and an online store. Billed as "the site where a dog can have its day,"

The Poop also has a "Pooppourri" section with links to topics ranging from "The Poop Pantry" (recipes to cook for one's dog) to "PoopaScopes" (doggie horoscopes).

www.ThePoop.com

Dogpile.com

While The Poop deals directly with dogs, if not actually their poop, Dogpile doesn't really address *any* canine topics. However, if you're searching the Web for an answer to a housetraining question — or a question on any other subject — Dogpile can help you get it. This "search engine of search engines" scours the Web's other cybersleuths to "fetch" you links to the information you need.

www.dogpile.com

Index